AF394545

Why

Korea?

The Unification of Korea
&
The Church's Mission
To Israel

Therese & Young Gil Gohng

Trafford Publishing

© Copyright 2006 Therese M. and Young Gil Gohng.
All rights reserved. No part of this publication may be reproduced, stored in a retrieval system, or transmitted, in any form or by any means, electronic, mechanical, photocopying, recording, or otherwise, without the written prior permission of the author.

Note for Librarians: A cataloguing record for this book is available from Library and Archives Canada at www.collectionscanada.ca/amicus/index-e.html
ISBN 1-4122-0178-0

Printed on paper with minimum 30% recycled fibre. Trafford's print shop runs on "green energy" from solar, wind and other environmentally-friendly power sources.

Offices in Canada, USA, Ireland and UK

This book was published *on-demand* in cooperation with Trafford Publishing. On-demand publishing is a unique process and service of making a book available for retail sale to the public taking advantage of on-demand manufacturing and Internet marketing. On-demand publishing includes promotions, retail sales, manufacturing, order fulfilment, accounting and collecting royalties on behalf of the author.

Book sales for North America and international:
Trafford Publishing, 6E–2333 Government St.,
Victoria, BC V8T 4P4 CANADA
phone 250 383 6864 (toll-free 1 888 232 4444)
fax 250 383 6804; email to orders@trafford.com

Book sales in Europe:
Trafford Publishing (UK) Limited, 9 Park End Street, 2nd Floor
Oxford, UK OX1 1HH UNITED KINGDOM
phone 44 (0)1865 722 113 (local rate 0845 230 9601)
facsimile 44 (0)1865 722 868; info.uk@trafford.com

Order online at:
trafford.com/05-3145

10 9 8 7 6 5 4 3 2 1

Contents

* All Scripture verses in this book, unless indicated otherwise, are quoted from the New King James Bible, 1990 edition.

What Prompted Me to Write This Book?

I was heartened when my daughter Mary told me how an American activist came to be involved in North Korea's human rights issue. I heard that the activist testified, "I confess I asked God a question: 'Why have you made North Korea such a central focus of my life with so much pain and suffering?' And God gently reminded me that many years ago I prayed to Him to break my heart for the things that broke His heart."

I was excited about what God did for her, but soon I began to question: *Why North Korea?* I know there are many suffering people in the world. Why should God be more concerned about North Koreans? Was it because they are the most oppressed people in the world? Does God deliver people in the order of how oppressed they are? I thought God would want to deliver all the people of the world from their suffering.

Although God is no doubt heartbroken because of the afflictions that North Koreans suffer, I thought there must be other reasons why God was so concerned about Korea.

My mind quickly swept through the prophecies in the book of Daniel. The prophecies of God must come to pass for the world and its inhabitants to be delivered from their suffering.

The book of Daniel is about how history is going to play out during the 'Age of Gentiles. The 'Age of Gentiles' is the period during which the Davidic King of Judah has been removed. It begins with the Babylonian Captivity of Israel and will end with the restoration of the Davidic King in the Kingdom of God on earth. So, we can say that we are still living in the Age of Gentiles.

According to the book of Daniel, there are four major empires during the Age of Gentiles that will rule Israel along with the known world of the time in relation to Israel. The known world of the time in relation to Israel was relatively smaller at the time of the first empire of Babylon. But it gradually expanded to encompass the whole world by the time of the fourth empire.

Babylon, Medo-Persia, and Greece were the first three Gentile empires that ruled Israel. The Scripture, however, described the fourth empire only as being, "dreadful and terrible and exceedingly strong; and it had huge iron teeth… It was different from all the beasts that were before it, and it had ten horns." (Dan. 7:7). It also says, "The fourth beast shall be a fourth Kingdom on earth, which shall…devour the *whole earth,* trample it and break it in pieces" (Dan. 7:23)

The fourth Kingdom which comprises entire Gentile nations began with the hegemony of the Roman Empire. It will go through five different stages from its beginning until the end: namely, the Roman Empire Stage, the Divided Stage, the Unified Stage, the Ten Kingdom Stage, and finally the Stage of Antichrist's Rule.

Although the fourth Kingdom may expand to control the entire earth for a while, it will eventually succumb to the Son of David and His Kingdom to bring the Age of Gentiles to its end.

The first stage, the Roman Empire Stage, will precipitate the second stage, the Divided Stage, which began with the division of the East and the West Rome. The Divided Stage will last long until it is finally replaced by the third stage, the Unified Stage, in the latter days. But the Unified Stage of the world will again divide into ten kingdoms to begin the fourth stage, which is called the Ten Kingdom Stage. At this point, Antichrist the lawless one will arise and devour three of the ten kingdoms and subjugate the remaining seven kingdoms under his control.

Technically, the world is still cruising through the Divided Stage because the Korean peninsula is still in division. The division of the Korean peninsula is a direct result of the East-West struggle, and the two Koreas in the peninsula can rightly be called its divided residual states.

As was mentioned earlier, the East-West struggle began with the division of the Roman Empire. The center of the East was Constantinople in the beginning, but it moved to Moscow when Constantinople was conquered by the Ottoman Empire in 1453. The leaders of the East fled to Russia, where they helped establishing "The Third Roman Empire of Russia." Although the Bolshevik Revolution in 1917 overthrew the Third Rome, the center of the East remained in Moscow. On the other hand, the center of the West began in Rome, but has been moved to Washington, D.C. through a tortuous course of history.

The disintegration of the Soviet Union was the decisive event that triggered the beginning of the Unified Stage, and the whole world is now waiting to see the Unified Stage of the world, when Kim Jong Il will be toppled from his reign of terror over North Korea.

However, the Unified Stage may not last long, according to the book of Daniel, and the world will soon be divided into ten kingdoms. We can conjecture that the developing economic blocs of today's nations may result in composing the ten kingdoms described in the book of Daniel. These latter-day events are developing so fast that we feel as if we are watching history on videotape. God seems to be expediting these events so that we may be delivered from our suffering sooner.

It is very reasonable to think that the divided residual states of the East-West struggle, the two Koreas, must be unified soon for the course of history to enter into the Unified Stage.

Now we may rightly guess that the fulfillment of the prophecy of God is another factor that God is so concerned about North Korea. If the prophecies were to be fulfilled sooner, North Korea and the whole world will come closer to the day of deliverance from the Evil One.

At this point, I still felt that God had to tell me another reason why He was so concerned about North Korea. Then,

I recalled the Paul's heartfelt solicitation to the Gentile believers, written in Romans 11:13-14:

> For I speak to you Gentiles; inasmuch as I am an apostle to the Gentiles, I magnify my ministry, if by any means I may provoke to godly jealousy[1] those who are my flesh and save some of them [the remnants].
>
> (Romans 11:13-14)

I know that the ultimate salvation of the world, with the arrival of the Kingdom on earth, cannot come without the fulfillment of these words because Jesus will not return to establish the Kingdom of God on the earth until Israel repents of her sin and seeks His return. When you learn what role Korea will play in carrying out the church's mission of arousing Israel to godly jealousy, you will come to understand why God is so concerned about Korea.

I thank God for what He showed to the American human rights activist, and I have also thanked for her obedience to

---

[1] This phrase in Romans 11:14 is controversial, because it is often translated with strong words like 'provoke to jealousy.' Since God called Himself 'a jealous God' nothing bad about is in the word 'jealousy' itself. Moreover, Paul said in II Corinthians 11:2, "For I am jealous for you with godly jealousy," when the Corinthian were misled by false teachers. So, we can safely assume that Paul meant that he wants to have his kinsmen aroused to godly jealousy, when he said, "If by any means I may provoke to jealously those who are my flesh and save some of them," KJV used 'emulation' in place of 'jealousy' to avoid misunderstanding. We translated it here as 'godly jealousy.'

God's calling. I thank God for her country, the United States of America, and I'm grateful to the American people for their willingness to sacrifice in faithfulness to the calling of God. I also thank God for choosing Korea to fulfill the last mission of the church.

I have lived to see World War II and the Korean War. I was still not quite 12 years old when World War II ended. In retrospect, I thought about the relationship between the United States and Korea, and about the providence of God. The United States first came to Korea way back in the latter part of nineteenth century to bring the gospel of Jesus Christ to its people. Then the liberation of Korea came as a result of World War II, and the United States was again involved in the Korean War to fight against our common enemy, communism.

I could not figure out the meaning of these wars and the suffering of the people at the time, but now I understand them because I came to know the One who is in control of the history of the world. I also realized how much Christians need to sacrifice, like Christ Jesus did, for the sake of the Kingdom. I remember what Peter said in I Peter 2:20-21: "But when you do good and suffer for it, if you take it patiently, this is commendable before God. For to this you were called, because Christ also suffered for us, leaving us an example, that you should follow His steps."

I have also come to know that Korea, though she may be corrupt and degraded now, will soon be cleansed, probably in the course of being unified, and will join the "Axis of God" as a valiant servant of God to take on the enemy of the Kingdom. It may take another book to elaborate on the concept of the "Axis of God," but what I mean by it in a few words is that Korea will be a part of the alliance of nations that will inevitably be formed in the course of history to confront the power of Antichrist, the "Axis of Evil."

God will deliver the suffering people in North Korea very soon and will save all mankind from the hands of the Evil One. Had it not been for the grace we have received, it certainly would be an onerous task to take on such an enemy. But we will prevail in God's love.

Young Gil Gohng
Nashua, NH
April 21, 2005

Introduction

The church is destined to finish its mission before the Church Age comes to an end. Many may think of the church's mission only in terms of spreading the gospel to the ends of the earth. It is true that this is one of the most important missions of the church, but there are two more important missions to finish during the Church Age. The Church Age began with the pouring out of the Holy Spirit on the day of Pentecost after Jesus' ascension and ends when the Rapture takes place.

The first mission of the church is to discipline believers to grow into the whole measure of the fullness of Christ. This was also said by our Lord Jesus Christ, at the table of the Last Supper as a commandment. He said to the disciples, "A new commandment I give to you, that you love one another; as I have loved you, that you also love one another. By this all will know that you are my disciples, if you have love for one another." (John 13:34-35).

Paul's teachings on the church in Ephesians 4:11-16 also elaborate on this theme as follows:

> And He Himself gave some to be apostles, some prophets, some evangelists, and some pastors and teachers, for the equipping of the saints for the work of ministry, for the edifying of the body of Christ, till we all come to the unity of the faith and the knowledge of the Son of God, to (become) a perfect man to

the measure of the stature of the fullness of Christ; that we should no longer be children, tossed to and fro and carried about with every wind of doctrine, by the trickery of men, in the cunning craftiness by which they lie in wait to deceive, but speaking the truth in love, may grow up in all things into Him who is the head—Christ—from whom the whole body, joined and knit together by what every joint supplies, according to the effective working by which every part does its share, causes growth of the body for the edifying of itself in love.

(Ephesians 4:11-16)

In Ephesians 5:26-27, Paul also envisioned what the church would be like when it stands before Jesus:

He might sanctify and cleanse it with the washing of water by the word, that He might present it to Himself a glorious church, not having spot or wrinkle or any such thing, but that it should be holy and without blemish.

(Ephesians 5:26-27)

The second mission is to preach the gospel to all nations until the full number of Gentiles has come in. The most prominent statements concerning the second mission of the church were made by Jesus Christ in Acts 1:8 and Mathew 28:18-20 as follows. These were His last words before leaving the earth for heaven.

But you shall receive power when the Holy Spirit has come upon you; and you shall be witnesses to Me in

> Jerusalem, and in all Judea and Samaria, and to the ends of the earth (Acts 1:8).
>
> All authority has been given to Me in heaven and earth. Go therefore and make disciples of all the nations, baptizing them in the name of the Father and the Son and the Holy Spirit, and teaching them to observe all things that I have commanded you; and lo, I am with you always, even to the end of the age. Amen. (Matt. 28:18-20).

The third and last mission of the church is to move Israel to godly jealousy so that she may accept Jesus as their Messiah. Jesus did not say this directly, but He alluded to it when He said to the Jewish people, "For I say to you, you shall see Me no more till you say, 'Blessed is He who comes in the name of the Lord'" (Matt. 23:39).

Jesus quoted this verse from Psalm 118:26, which essentially meant "You are my God, and I will praise You; You are my God, I will exalt You" as said below in verse 28 of the same Psalm. So, what Jesus said by quoting this verse was that the Jewish people will not see Him again until they praise and exalt Him as their Messiah and ask Him to return. We can see in the gospel that the believers of Jesus welcomed Him with this verse as He entered Jerusalem on a donkey as the King of Israel just before the feast of Passover.

God revealed the third mission clearly to Paul through the Holy Spirit later. This revelation is described in Romans 11:13-15:

For I speak to you Gentiles; inasmuch as I am an apostle to the Gentiles, I magnify my ministry, if by any means I may provoke to godly jealousy those who are my flesh and save some of them [the remnants]. For if their being cast away is the reconciling of the world, what will their acceptance be but life from the dead.

(Romans 11:13-15)

Israel was the first nation to hear the gospel because they were the chosen people and the first nation before God among the nations, but she did not accept it.

Paul, however, learned through a revelation that God had assigned the task of arousing Israel to godly jealousy to a Gentile nation so that Israel might come to accept the gospel of Jesus Christ. This is the third and last mission that we must complete before the Church Age comes to an end. The Scripture proves that the church was wrong in believing that Israel was banished because she refused to accept Jesus.

This small book is about the third mission of the church. For many years, the church has been misled on this issue, but now is the time to review it.

I. _________________

Apostle Paul's Burden For Israel

Even though Paul, the apostle to the Gentiles, poured forth his whole life to spread the Gospel among the Gentiles, he always carried a burden for the salvation of his kinsmen, the Israelites:

> I tell the truth in Christ, I am not lying, my conscience also bearing witness in the Holy Spirit, that I have great sorrow and continual grief in my heart. I could wish that I myself were accursed from Christ for my brethren, my kinsmen according to the flesh.
>
> (Romans 9:1-3)

After reading Paul's words, we can be assured that Paul cried out to God day and night with a great burden in his heart for his people. After such fervent entreaty, he finally received God's reply. God revealed to Paul the treasured secret that He had discreetly kept hidden lest anyone know of it before the time for the revelation came. That secret is God's amazing and prodigious plan for Israel's salvation. The apostle explains this in detail in chapters 9, 10, and 11 of Romans.

Astounded by God's profound plan for the salvation of Israel as it was made known to him through a revelation,

Paul could hardly withhold the overwhelming flow of joy and gratitude inspired by the Spirit, and thus he came to praise the Lord:

> Oh, the depth of the riches both of
>> The wisdom and knowledge of God!
>> How unseachable are His judgments:
>> And His ways past finding out!
> For who has known the mind of the Lord?
>> Or who has become His counselor
>> Or who has first given to Him
>> And it shall be repaid to Him?
> For of Him through Him and to Him
>> Are all things, to whom be glory forever, Amen.
>
> (Romans 11:33-35)

The great burden with which Paul started out ended in these words of immense joy and gratitude. The astounding plan, which so deeply moved the apostle, was God's profound providence to save Israel—Israel that had fallen and was seemingly in a state of utter hopelessness. Paul could not help being so moved because of the fact that the salvation of Israel was to be carried out through the Gentiles.

With such a great burden for Israel in his heart, Paul probably wanted time and again to devote himself totally to the work of leading his own people to salvation, even if it meant sacrificing his apostleship toward the Gentiles. Although tempted to leave, he had to collect his thoughts and reconfirm his apostleship toward the Gentiles. He had to see his work as a precious God-given mission and turn his heavy footsteps toward the Gentiles.

While he was in such agony, he realized one day through a revelation from God that the salvation of Israel was to come through the Gentiles and therefore his present work of spreading the gospel to the Gentiles was itself the initial step toward saving the Israelites. He came to the realization that what he was doing and what he had been doing up to that point was none other than the work to save his own brethren. The Scripture verse, "It shall come to pass that before they call, I will answer, and while they are still speaking, I will hear (Is. 65:24)," had indeed been realized. Even before Paul cried out, God already had this plan and was in the process of working it out. Therefore, Paul could not help but be more overwhelmed, grateful, and inspired. Now he could look upon his apostleship toward the Gentiles with more pride and honor. He is thus led to make this plea to the Gentile believers:

> For I speak to you Gentiles; inasmuch as I am an apostle to the Gentiles, I magnify my ministry, if by any means I may provoke to godly jealousy those who are my flesh and save some of them [the remnants].
> (Romans 11:13-14)

Now that he had come to the realization that the salvation of Israel depended upon whether the Gentiles could arose Israel to godly jealousy, he turned to make this heartfelt solicitation. He pleaded with the Gentiles to please not fail in saving "some of them," the remnants of Israel, by provoking Israel to godly jealousy by any means.

We cannot just bypass the apostle's fervent appeal upon hearing it. It is not simply because of its fervency or because we are the Gentiles, the fruit of Paul's hard labor for the Gentile church. Of course, we cannot forget our indebtedness to him, and we must do our best for the salvation of Israel to return what he has done for us. But the main reason we must cherish his plea in our hearts, recall it, and by all means make it come true is because it is the key by which the Kingdom of God will be established on earth. By reciting the Lord's Prayer from time to time, we call to mind that our main goal in life is to seek the Kingdom of God on earth: "Our Father in heaven, hollowed be Your Name, Your Kingdom come, Your will be done on earth as it is in heaven."

If the Kingdom of God cannot come, we have no other fate than to remain on this cursed earth as Satan's slaves, exploiting and being exploited by one another. This world is not a good place to live, even for atheists. This may be the reason why they also seek a utopia. Karl Marx could be said to be a leading figure among such atheists. But no matter how much research they do on history, society, and the physical realm, that utopia will never be realized until God lifts the curse that he has cast upon this earth. The utopia will never be realized through human research and efforts.

In the middle of twentieth century, people once had a high hope in science, and many believed that there was no limit to what science could do to turn this world into a paradise. It appeared the ideal society, where all human needs are met and all diseases are conquered or prevented, was just about within our reach, and optimism for our future prevailed. But very soon our top scientists and economists began to find out there is a limit to growth on this planet, due mainly to environmental pollution, shortage of resources, and rapid population growth. The tone of the outlook for the future of mankind has begun to change among scientists from optimism, confidence, and affluence to worry, anxiety, and frugality.

After the Renaissance, the fervor for utopia began to ferment during the late eighteenth and the early nineteenth centuries in Europe, also known as the Age of Reason. It was seen as a historical, natural process to replace the "paradise in the heaven" of the Middle Ages with a "utopia," as humanity gained confidence in human reason and its excellence, the ideal of humanism.

Karl Marx succeeded in formulating a powerful secular religion in the middle of the nineteenth century. Its bible, *The Communist Manifesto* gravitated toward realization of the utopia. The passion for Socialism and Marxism swept through all Europe for the rest of the nineteenth century and into the early twentieth century until finally, in 1917, the success of the Bolshevik Revolution made it possible for Russia to begin a serious attempt to build this utopia. The twentieth century was indeed an era in which mankind sought utopian societies on earth, through ideologies such as Fascism, Nazism, Communism, and so on.

However, it is extremely important to be aware that the origin of the secular attempt for utopia on earth is a direct challenge to God's plan of salvation and His Kingdom on earth. If we look back on the history of humanity, we find the first incident of an attempt by mankind to build a utopia on earth in Genesis chapter 11, the recorded history of the tower of Babel.

Then they said to one another, "Come, let us make bricks and bake them thoroughly." They had brick for stone, and they had asphalt for mortar. And they said, "Come, let us build ourselves a city and a tower whose top is in the heavens, let us make a name for ourselves, lest we be scattered abroad over the face of the whole earth."

(Genesis 11:3-4)

The tower whose top is in the heavens symbolizes the utopia that will match what only God can provide for mankind. Use of the bricks and asphalt in place of stones and mortar symbolizes the trust in human wisdom and crafts. They were building a heavenly place on the earth, relying upon their own wisdom and crafts to deliver them from the misery incurred by the Fall.

It was a real challenge to God's plan of salvation of the world. We can also see how Satan had preyed upon the pride of the fallen men from what they said. Instead of praising and glorifying God's name, they glorified their own names, saying, "Let us make a name for ourselves." Because of the human penchant for evil due to the temptation of Satan who has entered the world since the Fall, God had to stop their attempt to build the tower which would lead them to their own destruction, by a decisive action. The measure that God used was to confuse their language so that they might not be able to communicate to one another.

Right after the description of this event of Babel, Genesis narrates how God called Abraham to begin his work of salvation through the 'seed of woman,' which is the Messiah that He had promised in Genesis 3:15. This story is described in Genesis chapter 12 following the story of the tower of Babel in chapter 11.

It is not surprising to see that the spirit of Babel has revived in the form of Marxism as we approach the time for the Kingdom of God on earth. The spirit of Antichrist, which had been restrained at the event of Babel, is now in the process of being released after the Passion of Jesus. It was when Jesus finished his work of salvation on the cross. II Thessalonians 2:6-12 warns of Antichrist which is in the process of being released as follows:

> And now you know what is restraining, that he may be revealed in his own time. For the mystery of lawlessness is already at work; only He who now restrains will do so until He is taken out of the way. And then the lawless one will be revealed whom the Lord will consume with the breath of His mouth and destroy with the brightness of His coming. The coming of the lawless ones is according to the working of Satan, with all power, signs, and lying wonders, and with all unrighteous deception among those who perish, because they did not receive the love of truth, that they might be saved. And for this reason God will send them strong delusion, that they should believe lie, that they all may be condemned who did not believe the truth but had pleasure in unrighteousness.
>
> (II Thessalonians 2:6-12)

From this passage of Scripture, we can imagine what it will be like when the Lord's power, which now holds back, is taken out of the way and the lawless one is fully revealed. The lawless one will manifest itself with signs and wonders to deceive those who have pleasure in unrighteousness. Satan will do everything he can to thwart God's plan of salvation and to delude people into believing in what he offers.

Moreover, when Satan realized that people had come to know the limits of the physical sciences, he began to promote the pseudo-spiritual forms, such as ESP, psychic powers, the new age movement, and so on, to continue his work of deception. But he labors in vain. See what God says about the Satan's challenge:

> Why do nations rage and people plot a vain thing? The kings of the earth set themselves, and the rulers take counsel together, against the Lord and against His anointed, saying, "Let us break Their bonds in pieces and cast away Their cords from us." He who sits in the heavens shall laugh; the Lord shall hold them in derision. Then He shall speak to them in His wrath. And distress them in His deep displeasure; yet I have set My King on My holy hill of Zion.
>
> (Psalms 2:1-6)

The Millennial Kingdom of God described in the Scripture is a stage toward the eternal Kingdom of God. Yet, we know through the description of it in the book of Isaiah and some other books of prophets that it surpasses by far the utopian society that mankind ever dreamed of. Jesus will complete the eternal Kingdom on earth after one thousand years of the Messianic Kingdom has passed. This is in fact what God has promised in the covenant with Abraham.

The Scripture verse, "But seek first the Kingdom of God and His righteousness. (Matt. 6:33)" reminds us that our attitude toward living in this world should be self sacrificing so we can bring about that Kingdom. The Scripture also says, "If anyone desires to come after Me, let him deny himself, and take up His cross and follow me; For whoever desires to save his life will lose it, and whoever loses his life for My sake will find it (Matthew.16:24-25)."

We should be prepared to lay down our lives if needed, to move Israelites to godly jealousy and usher them in to their Messiah, Jesus Christ.

II.

Why the Kingdom of God Will Never Come Unless Israel Returns to Jesus Christ

Why is it that the Kingdom will never come to fruition unless Israel acknowledges her offense of rejecting Christ and returns to Him?

In the first advent, Jesus proclaimed and proved He was the Son of God, the Messiah, by performing miracles that no one had done before Jesus came. The rabbis traditionally taught that when the Messiah came, He would heal the leper, cast out the demons that caused deafness, and open the eyes of the blind. Since only the Messiah would be able to perform such miracles, when such a one appeared, the Jewish people were to recognize him as the Messiah. This is why, when John the Baptist sent his disciples to Jesus to ask whether He was really the promised Messiah, Jesus replied, "Go and tell John the things which you see and hear. The blind receive their sight and the lame walk; the lepers are cleansed and the deaf hear; the dead are raised up and the poor have the gospel preached to them. And blessed is he who is not offended because of Me."

If one considers the sequence of miracles in the synoptic gospels, the first Messianic miracle that Jesus performed seems to have been the healing of a leper. Leviticus 13 and 14 detail the regulations for diagnosing and isolating lepers, the necessary steps for cleansing the impurity after it is healed, and what offerings are required afterward. But since there was no case in which the rabbis themselves had healed a leper, these regulations for a healed leper had never been used. They believed that these regulations would be of use when the Messiah came.

In the Old Testament, Moses' prayer healed his sister Miriam, and the Syrian general Naaman was healed by Elisha. But in both of these cases, the regulations in Leviticus could not be applied.

In Miriam's case, the regulations were not applicable because it was before the Israelites entered Canaan, which was the time set for the regulations to be applied, according to Leviticus 14:34: "When you have come into the land of Canaan, which I give you as a possession, and I put the leprous plague in a house in the land of your possession." And in Naaman's case, these regulations were not applied because he was a Gentile.

But in the gospel we see that Jesus healed a leper and ordered that these regulations be carried out for the first time since they were given:

> Then He put out His hand and touched him saying, "I am willing; be cleansed!" And immediately the leprosy left him. And He charged him to tell no one, "But go and show yourself to the priest, and make an

offering for your cleansing, as a testimony to them, just as Moses commanded." Then the report went around concerning Him all the more; and great multitudes came together to hear, and to be healed by Him of their infirmities. So He Himself withdrew into the wilderness and prayed.

(Luke 5:13-16)

Jesus performed this miracle to prove to the leaders of Israel that He was the Messiah and ordered that the healed leper go and testify before the priests. Then Jesus retreated into the wilderness to pray at this crucial moment in His public ministry, when He had taken His first step to announce that He was the Messiah. He probably wanted to pray for the priests, who would witness the healing of the leprosy, and also hear from the Father as to what he should be doing next.

The Israelites despised Nazareth, so when a Nazarene healed a leper, it was a big event. They immediately called the Sanhedrin into session and decided to discern this leprosy-healing case according to their regulation.

The Sanhedrin's regulations to discern cases like this comprised three stages. The first stage was to go through a close observation of the performance, the 'stage of observation.' This would be followed by the 'stage of questioning' and then the 'stage of final discernment' in the meeting of the Sanhedrin. We can find the 'stage of observation' in operation in the healing case of the paralytic recorded in Luke 5:17-26.

> Now it happened on a certain day, as He was teaching that there were Pharisees and teachers of the law sitting by, who had come out of every town of Galilee, Judea and Jerusalem. And the power of the Lord was present to heal them.
>
> (Luke 5:17-26)

Pharisees and teachers of the law from every town of Galilee, Judea, and Jerusalem were gathered from all over the country. The reason why all the leaders were gathered from throughout the country can be ascribed to the Sanhedrin's decision to have the leaders observe the works of Jesus. According to Mark 2:1, this event took place in Capernaum. Naturally, they came from every village from the Galilee district where Capernaum is located, but also from all over Judea and Jerusalem to make their observation. The leaders that came from Jerusalem were probably dispatched directly from the Sanhedrin.

Jesus, being aware of the presence of the leaders, healed the paralytic with these unusual words: "Man, your sins are forgiven." He thus proved that He was the Son of God, the Messiah, so that they could not deny Him. Since the Pharisees and teachers of the law knew that only God could forgive sin, it was only reasonable that they should have acknowledged that Jesus was the Son of God after seeing Him perform the healing miracle by the forgiving of sin.

But they took it as blasphemy instead. It is recorded that they thought to themselves as follows:

> And the scribes and the Pharisees began to reason, saying, "Who is this who speaks blasphemies? Who can forgive sins but God alone?"
>
> (Luke 5:21)

The reason why the scribes didn't as yet speak directly to Jesus but only thought in themselves was because they were still in the observation stage prior to the questioning stage. But they soon began direct questioning and started to pick on Him. One can find a plethora of these incidents throughout the gospels. Those incidences are found in the Jesus' encounters with Pharisees during the period after Jesus healed the leper and before He was condemned by the Sanhedrin. The most prominent one is the healing of a sick man at the pool of Bethesda as described in John 5:1-47. The Jews picked on Him and sought to kill him because He healed the sick on the day of Sabbath and called God His Father. They also accused Him of associating with sinners like tax collectors and prostitutes, and of His disciples not fasting.

Finally, we find the incident where they declare the decision of Sanhedrin on the healing of the leper in Matthew chapter 12:

> Then one was brought to Him who was demon-possessed, blind and mute; and He healed him, so that the blind and mute man both spoke and saw. And all the multitudes were amazed and said, "Could this be the Son of David?" But when the Pharisees heard it they said, "This fellow does not cast out de-

mons except by Beelzebub, the ruler of the demons."

(Matthew 12:22-24)

The crowd that witnessed this miracle recognized Jesus as the Messiah, declaring, "Could this be the Son of David?" They knew through the Scripture that the Messiah to come was the Son of David. So they were affirming to themselves that this man must be the awaited Son of David, the Messiah. But the Pharisees were different. They accused Jesus of casting out demons by Beelzebub. By this time the Sanhedrin had already come to the decision to deny that He was the Messiah, and it declared its decision on this occasion. How could they know that this decision would scatter the Israelites among Gentile nations, even today, thus determining the life of Diaspora?

Jesus listened to their decision and condemned it.

> Therefore I say to you, every sin and blasphemy will be forgiven men, but the blasphemy against the Spirit will not be forgiven men. Anyone who speaks a word against the Son of Man will be forgiven him; but whoever speaks against the Holy Spirit, it will not be forgiven him, either in this age or in the age to come. Either make the tree good and its fruit good or else make the tree bad and its fruit bad; for a tree is known by its fruit.

(Matthew 12:31-33)

Since the Son of Man came in the form of a human being, it is pardonable if one recognizes Him only as a human being and rejects Him. But if one rejects Him even after witnessing the work of the Holy Spirit, such as this, then it is the same as rejecting the Holy Sprit and therefore unpardonable. How can a bad tree bear good fruit? How can a bad tree bear the good fruit of healing by casting out a deaf-mute demon? Jesus is the tree that bears the fruit of life. To make a good tree seem like a bad tree, they say that the miracle came from the Devil. So Jesus made it clear that this sin is unpardonable in this age or the age to come.

Indeed, this sin was not forgiven in this age, and Israel was destroyed in A.D. 70 after a Roman Army led by General Titus besieged Jerusalem. In this war as many as 1.1 million Israelites were killed and approximately 97,000 were taken and sold as slaves. In A.D. 135 they were completely banished from that land by Emperor Hadrian and an order was pronounced prohibiting their reentrance. Even the name of Jerusalem was changed, and it was called Aelia Capitolina from then on. Thus began the Jewish life of the Diaspora, wandering among nations without a country.

This historic fact is the realization of what Jesus said in Luke 19:41-44:

> Now as He drew near, He saw the city and wept over it, saying, "If you had known, even you, especially in this your day, the things that make for your peace! But now they are hidden from your eyes. For the days will come upon you when your enemies will build an embankment around you, surround you and close you in on every side, and level you, and your children within you to the ground; and they will not leave in you one stone upon another, because you did not know the time of your visitation.
>
> (Luke 19:41-44)

Gazing at Jerusalem, which truly did not know what would bring her peace and did not recognize the time of God's coming, Jesus prophesied these words:

> O! Jerusalem, Jerusalem, the one who kills the prophets and stones those who are sent to her! How often I wanted to gather your children together, as a hen gathers her chicks under her wings, but you were not willing! See! Your house (the Lord's house) is left to you desolate; for I say to you, you shall see Me no more till you say, "Blessed is He who comes in the name of the Lord!"
>
> (Matthew 23:37-39)

The words, "For I say to you, you shall see Me no more till you say, 'Blessed is He who comes in the name of the Lord!'" are the answer to the question of why the Kingdom of God cannot come until Israel repents.

The verse is the Jewish praise for welcoming the Messiah, as we find in the gospel that the Jews who believed in Jesus welcomed Him when He entered Jerusalem on a donkey by saying, "Hosanna to the Son of David! Blessed is He who comes in the name of the Lord! Hosanna in the highest! (Matt. 21:9)" This is a scene in which the believers in Jesus welcome Him as their Messiah. The verse is, as previously explained above, a quotation from Psalm 118:26.

Therefore, when Jesus said, "You shall see Me no more till you say, 'Blessed is He who comes in the name of the Lord,'" He meant that He will not come back to the earth until the Jews acknowledge their guilt, seek Him as their Messiah, and welcome Him.

God also spoke earlier through the prophet Hosea:

> I will return again to My place (heaven) till they acknowledge their offence. Then, they will seek My face in their affliction. They will diligently seek Me. "Come, and let us return to the Lord; for He has torn but He will heal us; He has stricken but He will bind us up. After two days He will revive us; on the third day He will raise us up, that we may live in His sight, Let us know, let us pursue the knowledge of the Lord; His going forth is established as the morning, He will come to us like the rain, like the latter and former rain to the earth."
>
> (Hosea 5:15-6:3)

These words through Hosea mean that Jesus will return to 'His place in heaven, and will wait until Israel repents of her offense of not accepting Jesus and seeks His face.

Peter also confirms this fact in Acts 3:14-21 as follows:

> "But you denied the Holy One and the Just and asked for a murderer to be granted to you, and killed the Prince of life, whom God raised from the dead, of which we are witnesses... Repent therefore and be converted, that your sins may be blotted out, so that 'times of refreshing'[2] may come from the presence of the Lord, and that He may send Jesus Christ, who was preached to you before, whom heaven must receive until the times of restoration of all things,

---

[2]   The 'times of refreshing' is an expression used in the early church to denote the 'Kingdom of God on earth.'

which God has spoken by the mouth of all His holy prophets since the world began. . . "

(Acts 3:14-21)

God has spoken through the prophet Hosea that Jesus would wait 'till they acknowledge their offence.' Jesus knew that Israelites would seek Him in the last days when they would be under attack by Antichrist during the tribulation. This is described in Zechariah 12:2, 3, 10 as follows:

> Behold I will make Jerusalem a cup of drunkenness to all the surrounding peoples, when they lay siege against Judah and Jerusalem. And it shall happen in that day that I will make Jerusalem a very heavy stone for all peoples; all who would heave it away will surely be cut in pieces, though all nations of the earth are gathered against it... And I will pour on the house of David and on the inhabitants of Jerusalem the Spirit of grace and supplication; then they will look on Me whom they have pierced; they will mourn for Him as one mourns for his only son, and grieve for Him as one grieves for a firstborn.
>
> (Zechariah: 12:2, 3, 10)

Although the leaders who misled the people and rejected Jesus were small in number, theirs was a national sin because they represented the nation of Israel. Therefore, if Israel's leaders in the future do not repent and ask Jesus on behalf of the nation to return, He will not come again, and in such case the Kingdom of God will never be realized on earth.

If so, Jesus' second coming will depend upon whether Israel will repent. And again, it will depend upon whether the Gentiles are able to arouse Israel to jealousy. For this reason we must do our utmost in arousing Israel to godly jealousy so that she may come to accept Christ Jesus as their Messiah.

God not only makes plans but also gives the means to achieve those plans—our prayers and obedience. God's plans for men cannot be accomplished on this earth without our prayers and obedience.

III.

Paul's Concern for the Gentiles Who Are to Arose Israel to Godly Jealousy

In His wondrous way, God turned the misfortune of the Israelites' unbelief into a blessing by making it an opportunity to save all of mankind. God has used the unbelief of Israel as his chance to spread the gospel among the Gentiles, and in turn, the Gentiles will arouse Israel to godly jealousy so that they may return to Christ. Thus, the whole of mankind may be saved.

Paul explains in Romans 11:11-15 that if the stumbling of Israel brings blessing and salvation to the Gentiles and the reconciliation of the world, "what will their acceptance be but life from the dead?"

> I say then, have they stumbled that they should fall? Certainly not! But through their fall, to provoke them to godly jealousy, salvation has come to the Gentiles. Now if their fall is riches for the world, and their failure riches for the Gentiles, how much more their fullness! For I speak to you Gentiles; inasmuch as I am an apostle to the Gentiles, I magnify my ministry, if by any means I may provoke to godly jealousy those who are my flesh and save some of them [the

"remnants"]. For if their being cast away is the reconciling of the world, what will their acceptance be but life from the dead?

(Romans 11:11-15).

By "life from the dead," he meant the resurrected life in the Kingdom of God, because the repentance of Israel and her acceptance of Christ will cause Jesus to return to the earth and establish His Kingdom.

Paul gives the reasons why we can be assured of the salvation of the Gentiles and Israel in Romans 11:28-32:

Concerning the gospel they are enemies for your sake, but concerning the election they are beloved for the sake of the fathers. For the gifts and calling of God are irrevocable. For as you were once disobedient to God, yet have now obtained mercy through their disobedience, even so these also have now been disobedient, that through the mercy shown you they also may obtain mercy. For God has committed them all to disobedience, that He might have mercy on all.

(Romans 11:28-32)

Although Israel's refusal to accept the gospel made them enemies of believers, they are beloved of God because of His election of their fathers—and there is no change in this as determined by God in His plan. Just as the Gentiles were once disobedient to God but were saved through God's mercy as a result of Israel's disobedience, so God will bestow mercy on Israel and save them through His mercy shown to the Gentiles. The reason why God left both Israel and the Gentiles in disobedience for a period of time was because it was His plan to save them by bestowing His grace on both the Israelites and the Gentiles.

Israel is by no means ruined fully to the end—they have merely stumbled temporarily. While they were in a fallen state, God first saved the Gentiles by having the gospel preached to them and then through these Gentiles He will also save Israel.

The expression "life from the dead" is used to signify the Kingdom of God that we will inherit when Israel returns to God. "Life from the dead" aptly expresses in a few words the image of the restored Kingdom as written in the books of Isaiah and Micah as follows:

> Now it shall come to pass in the latter days that the mountain of the Lord's house shall be established on the top of the mountains, and shall be exalted above the hills; and all nations shall flow to it. Many peoples shall come and say, "Come, let us go up to the mountain of the Lord, to the house of the God of Jacob. He will teach us His ways, and we shall pass in His paths." For out of Zion shall go forth the law and the word of the Lord from Jerusalem. He shall judge between the nations, and shall rebuke many people; they shall beat their swords into plowshares, and their spears into pruning hooks; nation shall not lift up sword against nation, neither shall they learn war anymore.

> O house of Jacob, come and let us walk in the light of the Lord. For You have forsaken Your people, the house of Jacob, because they are filled with eastern ways; they are soothsayers like the Philistines, and they

are pleased with the children of foreigners. Their land is also full of silver and gold, and there is no end to their treasures; their land is also full of horses, and there is no end to their chariots. Their land is also full of idols; they worship the work of their own hands, that which their own fingers have made. People bow down, and each man humbles himself; therefore do not forgive them.

Enter into the rock, and hide in the dust, from the terror of the Lord and the glory of His majesty. The lofty looks of man shall be humbled, the haughtiness of men shall be bowed down, and the Lord alone shall be exalted in that day.

> For the day of the Lord of hosts shall come upon everything proud and lofty, upon everything lifted up—and it shall be brought low—upon all the cedars of Lebanon that are high and lifted up, and upon all the oaks of Bashan; upon all the high mountains, and upon all the hills that are lifted up; upon every high tower, and upon every fortified wall; upon all the ships of Tarshish, and upon all the beautiful sloops. The loftiness of man shall be bowed down, and the haughtiness of men shall be brought low; The Lord alone will be exalted in that day, but the idols He shall utterly abolish.

They shall go into the holes of the rocks, and into the caves of the earth, from the terror of the Lord and the glory of His Majesty, when He arises to shake the earth mightily.

> Sever yourselves from such a man, whose breath is in his nostrils; for of what account is he? (Is. 2:2-22)
>
> Everyone shall sit under his vine and under his fig tree, and no one shall make them afraid; for the mouth of the Lord of hosts has spoken. . .(Micah 4:4).
> They will not hurt nor destroy in all My holy mountain, for the earth shall be full of the knowledge of the Lord as the water cover the sea. (Is. 11:9)
>
> (Isaiah 2:2-22; Micah 4:4; Isaiah 11:9)

These Scripture describes what it will be like when the world is judged and the curse lifted from it. In other words, it is a restoration of life and a "life from the dead."

We see, however, that Paul's concern shifts from his kinsmen to the Gentiles. He is unsure whether the Gentiles will be capable of arousing Israel to godly jealousy. He guessed that if the Gentiles fail in doing this, the probable cause would be their arrogance due to Israel's failure and the Gentiles' success, and he calls special attention to this fact in Romans 11:16-18:

> For if the first fruit is holy, the lump is also holy; and if the root is holy, so are the branches. And if some of the branches were broken off, and you, being a wild olive tree, were grafted in among them, and with them became a partaker of the root and fatness of the olive tree, do not boast against the branches. But if you boast, remember that you do not support the root, but the root supports you.
>
> (Romans 11:16-18)

Reasoning that there was a danger for the Gentiles to become proud as they forgot their true position, Paul explained the relationship between Israel and the Christian Gentiles in the context of the history of salvation.

He likened the root of a tree to the first fruit offered to God in the Feast of the First Fruit, and said that if the root was holy, so were the branches just as the first fruit makes the lump holy in the Feast. What Paul was essentially saying was that the promise that Israel's forefather Abraham received through the covenant with God, was like the root of the tree of Israel. So, the root of Israel would make the branches holy just as the first fruit offered to God in the Feast of the First Fruit would make the whole lump holy. This, of course, must be true when the branches also hold on to the faith in the promise given to Abraham.

Paul then points out that the Gentiles are like the wild olive tree which has been grafted into the root of the tree of Israel. Without the holy root, there cannot be holy branches. Even though part of the branch, meaning most of the unbelieving Israelites, has fallen off, leaving the branch broken, the tree is still the tree of Israel and the wild olive tree grafted into the tree is sustained by the rich sap from the root of that tree of Israel. Since the relationship between the salvation of the Gentiles and Israel is such, the Gentiles are in no position to be conceited over the broken branch.

> You may say then, "The branches were broken off that I might be grafted in." Well said. Because of unbelief they were broken off, and you stand by faith. Do not be haughty, but fear. For if God did not spare the natural branches, He may not spare you either.

Therefore, consider the goodness and severity of God: on those who fell, severity; but toward you, goodness if you continue in His goodness. Otherwise, you also will be cut off.

Romans 11:19-22)

If one believes that Israel was broken off so that the Gentiles might be grafted in, this should never be a cause to make one proud. But rather it should be a lesson that we, in fear, should be careful that we are not cut off. God is not only a God of mercy, but He is also a God of severity. To those who are obedient, He is merciful, but to those who are proud and disobedient, He is severe.

Therefore, it is Paul's plea for the Gentiles to be by all means humble and obedient so as not to be cut off but to become Gentiles that can arouse Israel to godly jealousy. Then, Paul asserts, Israel will be restored when she comes to believe in Jesus Christ:

And they also, if they do not continue in unbelief will be grafted in, for God is able to graft them in again. For if you were cut out of the olive tree which is wild by nature, and were grafted contrary to nature into a good olive tree, how much more will these, who are the natural branches, be grafted into their own olive tree? For I do not desire, brethren, that you should be ignorant of this mystery, lest you should be wise in your own opinion, that hardening in part has happened to Israel until the fullness of the Gentiles has come in. And so all Israel will be saved, as it is written:

43

"The deliverer will come out of Zion,
And He will turn away ungodliness from
Jacob; for this is my covenant with them when
I take away their sins."

(Romans 11:23-27)

If Israel turns away from her unbelief and accepts Jesus, she will be restored even more easily and aptly than the Gentiles. God is able to do this. It is His plan to save Israel after a number of saved Gentiles are filled. By "all Israel," he meant all of the remnants of Israel—that is, the whole of Israel as a nation.

IV.

How Has the Church Done So Far in Arousing Israel To Godly Jealousy?

Let us look back on church history to see whether Paul's anxious concern was uncalled for. In the two thousand years of its history, has the church been able to arouse godly jealousy in Israel? Has the church been able to show the Jewish people the same mercy that God has shown to them, as Paul solicited? Has the church actually been an object of jealousy to Israel? Has any single Christian nation ever been an object of envy to them? It is sad to say 'no,' but it is true. The church, on the contrary, has provoked the Jewish people to anger and contempt.

How does a nation provoke Israel to jealousy? To provoke Israel to jealousy, a Christian nation must do what is rightly the calling of Israel—to spread the justice and love of God, as the prophets told us, throughout the world. When Israel sees this, she will become envious and repent on her own for her failure to stir herself up so that she herself may spread the justice and love of God.

There are some who have the wrong idea about this. They think the church has already provoked Israel to godly jealousy by accepting the gospel. If this were really the case, Paul would not have made such heartfelt pleas to the Gentiles to stir Israel to jealousy; and there would have been no need for him to be so burdened. If one followed this line of thinking, the Gentiles would simply seem mistaken from a Jewish point of view, for they have picked up what Israel herself had thrown away.

There are also some who think Israel is provoked to jealousy because Christian nations and Christian leaders are leading the world today. Jews are not naïve. They know that the whole world is now biblically going through the Age of Gentiles, and it will last until the Son of David finally comes to rule the world. They have watched many Gentile empires dominate the world, from Egypt and Assyria down to Babylon, Medo-Persia, Greece, and Rome, while they themselves have survived under their reigns.

They also observed the rise of Rome and its Christianizing process down to the prosperity of powerful Christian empires, such as the Frank Holy Roman Empire, the Germanic Holy Roman Empire, Spain, Great Britain, the Third Roman Empire of Russia under the czars, and so on. They have witnessed through direct encounter with these empires that the principle of their prosperity was by nature not any different from that of the preceding powers.

Their prosperity did not seem to be based on God's justice and love, even though they were Christian empires, but based more on violence and extortion. The Israelites, who know what is written in the Scripture, could not have loved such empires. On the contrary, those nations must have been the objects of her disillusionment, resentment, contempt, and derision.

Of course, it would not be fair if only their wrongdoings were castigated in this manner, because the Christians in those empires, making use of their nation's resources, did their best to spread the gospel of Jesus Christ throughout the world. Even in the Christian empires, weeds have grown along with the wheat, as predicted by Jesus.

The birth of the United States of America in 1776 marked a new era of enlightenment in the history of mankind. This nation, from its beginning, has struggled to be one that trusts in God and carries out the love and the justice of God on earth.

The United States came to being when slavery was still a norm. Nevertheless, she had the courage to declare the equality of all mankind before God in her Declaration of Independence, because the founding fathers knew what God had in His mind and what was right in the sight of God.

Despite the fact that the United States had discrimination against races until very recent years, no one can deny that the United States has played a very important role in abolishing discrimination against races and expanding freedom and human rights throughout her history. She has been a beacon on the hill for freedom and democracy for the people of the world since her inception.

The role that the United States has played after World War II is indeed epoch making and impressive. No such thing as Marshall Plan had ever been seen in the history of mankind before the United States. The United States assisted her fallen enemies to rebuild their destroyed homelands and economies instead of levying the compensation of the war.

The fact that mankind is learning to love one another and uphold the truth of God more and more as history approaches its end days gives us a hope that we may somehow, with God's grace, be able to build a just and loving nation that may be able to arouse Israel to godly envy so that she may also come back to Jesus Christ.

However, those who have a ministry to bring the gospel to Israel all agree that the word "Christian" should never be used when preaching the gospel to them, for the word "Christian" reminds them of all kinds of Jewish massacres and atrocities perpetrated by the Christian Church and even Hitler. We were told that a clergyman visiting Israel was spat on while walking the streets. Why is it that Christians, who are supposed to make Israel jealous and envious, are considered to be of such ill repute? Indeed, Paul's apprehension was by no means uncalled for. The fact that Christians, in the name of Christ, perpetrated such heinous crimes against Jews by persecuting and massacring them was probably because they did not understand the meaning of Paul's heartfelt pleas in Romans, or they purposefully distorted their meaning.

Although Israel was severely suppressed by such nations as Egypt, Assyria, Babylon, Persia, Greece, and Rome, they were still better off than they were under the Christian nations or the church. If one can say that Israel had a history of being dominated and suppressed by these nations, the relation between Israel and the church or the Christian nations can rightly be said as a history of being massacred by them. We remember the merciless massacre of Jews by Hitler, but it would be wrong to put all the blame on Hitler and Germany. In fact, the responsibility first lay in the church.

Let us go back to the Third Lateran Council of the Catholic Church in A.D. 1179 and recall the decisions of that council. The council's decisions forbade Jews to employ Christians and prohibited Jews and Christians from inhabiting the same household, thus officially discriminating against Jews for the first time in church history.

Later, in 1215, the Fourth Lateran Council, held under Pope Innocent III, stressed that the decisions of the Third Lateran Council should be more strictly enforced and committed an even bigger crime by adding the following four inhumane decisions:

1. Jews are not allowed to hold public office. Anyone who grants a public office to a Jew will be excommunicated.

2. Jews are not allowed to come out of their house on Easter Sunday but must stay indoors with the door shut.

3. All Jews must pay the Jewish tax (a new tax that Jews must pay because they are Jews).

4. All Jews must wear a badge and particular hat to show that they are Jews.

The yellow badge that Hitler forced Jews to wear was not his invention but originated in the church. Such decisions by the Lateran Council later influenced Christians to be crueler to the Jews and backed up the numerous Jewish massacres in the thirteenth and fourteenth centuries.

In line with the spirit of the Lateran Councils, the formation of the first ghetto in Venice, Italy, was initiated by the bull of Pope Paul IV. The word ghetto today is used to signify Jewish slum, but it was originally a special zone segregated from the rest of the city by walls and gates where Jews were ordered to live to discriminate against them. The Jews were not allowed to come outside the ghettos on Sundays and Christian holidays.

Also, the massacres of Jewish people by the crusaders left an indelible blemish on the history of the church. What the crusades ostensibly advocated was the recovery of the Holy Land from the Muslims, but from such a goal was naturally deduced spirit which claimed "If we are to liberate Jerusalem from the infidel Muslims, should we not first punish those who killed Christ?"

In a letter from Pope Innocent III to Louis VII of France, the Pope reveals his inmost thoughts by these remarks:

> What would it profit to fight against enemies of the cross in remote lands, while the wicked Jews, who blaspheme Christ, and who are much worse than the Saracens, go free and unpunished? Much more are the Jews to be execrated and hated than the Saracens: for the latter accept the birth of the Virgin, but the Jews deny it and blaspheme the doctrine and all Christian mysteries. God does not want them to be

wholly exterminated, but to be kept, like the fratricide Cain for still more severe torment and disgrace.
In this way God's most just severity has dealt with the Jews from the time of Christ's passion and will continue to deal with them to the end of the world, for they are accursed, and deserve to be.

(These historical facts narrated above so far are from *'History of the Christian Church'* by Schaff, P. 1996)

On their way to conquer Jerusalem, the Crusaders attacked Jewish communities in numerous places and massacred them in the name of Christ. Meanwhile, in the rear, not only were massacres perpetrated all over the place in the name of Christ under the leadership of priests and monks, but the Crusaders even had a slogan saying, "Save your soul by killing a Jew. By that merit shorten your stay in purgatory." When they finally occupied Jerusalem during their first expedition, they captured all the Jews living in Jerusalem, swept them into the synagogue, and annihilated them all by setting the synagogue on fire.

During the two hundred years of the Crusades, the Jews were endlessly attacked and massacred by the Christians. They even had to change their system of genealogy because Jewish women were the victims of numerous rapes. Originally, if the father of a child was a Jew, the child was considered a Jew in the Jewish genealogical system, even if it was born of a Gentile mother. But many illegitimate children were born with indefinite fathers because of rapes committed by the Crusaders, and thus the system was changed so that if the mother was a Jew, the child was recognized to be a Jew.

Moreover, if any unfortunate situation arose, it was a habitual practice of Christians and the church to put the blame on Jews and kill them as scapegoats. For instance, when the Black Death epidemic spread through the land, Christians accused the Jews of contaminating their wells and attacked Jewish communities to slaughter them. When the plague spread, it is said that the death rate of Jews was lower than that of the Gentiles, and this was because by their practice of the Mosaic Law they lived a comparatively sanitary life. But the Christians took this as evidence that the Jews had polluted their wells.

When a child was missing, Christians would accuse Jews of kidnapping him to put the child's blood in the matzos to be used for the Passover feast. Cardinal Carafa, who later became Pope Paul IV, even blamed the Jews for causing Luther's Reformation and ordered the burning of the Talmud and all books in Hebrew, as many as they could lay hands on. When twenty-five Moranos were discovered, he had them burned alive. Moranos were Jews in Spain who became Catholics by force, not being able to withstand the persecution by the church. But they were Christians only in appearance and kept their Jewish faith underground.

The church even fabricated plots to have the Jews massacred. One of the most well-known examples is the case where Christians would nail the wafer used during Holy Communion to a tree and accuse Jews of stealing the wafer from the church and nailing it to a tree to nail Christ to the cross again. According to the Catholic doctrine, when the wafer is consecrated, it becomes the body of Christ. So Catholics call a consecrated wafer the "Host" and consider it the equivalent of Jesus. To them, nailing the Host is the same as nailing Christ.

How did the Reformed church treat the Jews? Luther at first pointed out the wrong the Catholic Church had done to the Jews. He said that the Catholic Church was to blame for the Jews not believing in Christ, and expected them to be converted into the Reformed Church. But when they didn't show any changed response toward the Reformed Church, he circulated a leaflet asserting that their synagogues, houses, and books should be burned and that they should be driven out of Germany and not be allowed to have professions in medicine or commerce, thus setting the Reformed church on an anti-Semitic path.

It is said that he delivered a sermon in his hometown a few days before his death in 1545, stating that the Jews should be purged from Germany for they were a dangerous enemy to the Christians. Due to his influence, protestant Europe also forced the Jews to live in ghettoes and to wear yellow badges and yellow hats. In their attitude toward the Jews, the Catholic Church and the Reformed Church can be considered basically the same in their anti-Semitism.

What does the church have to say to the Jewish people today after it has perpetrated such injustice and heinous crimes? The church certainly has not been able to arouse the Jewish people to godly jealousy but instead has angered them, as did the foolish nation of Babylon.

Romans 10:19 quotes Deuteronomy 32:21b, saying, "I will provoke you to godly jealousy by those who are not My people (the Gentiles); I will anger you by a foolish nation."

We know through this verse that two kinds of Gentile nations are involved throughout history. One nation will arouse Israel to godly jealousy for emulation and the other one will provoke Israel to anger. The Christian nations should never be the object of Israel's anger and derision, but by all means should be the object of Israel's godly envy.

V. _______________________

Satan's Plot:

The Name of Israel May Be Remembered No More

Satan's scheme lies behind the massacre of Jews perpetrated by the church. Satan, by using the church as his instrument in persecuting Jews, contrived to achieve a double purpose. By having the Jews persecuted and massacred in the name of Christ, Satan effectively prevented the Jews from becoming Christians. He used the church not only to annihilate the Jews but also to make them eschew Christianity altogether. Satan knows if his scheme were to be successful, he could hold onto the earth forever because there would be no Jews left to plead for Christ's return. As previously explained Jesus will not return unless the Jews repent of their sin and beseech for His return. It is now clear that the church and the Christians have been deceived by Satan's scheme.

Adam, who was deceived by Satan, sinned and lost his right over the earth and all the creatures on it. But Jesus restored this right through his death on the cross, repaying the price of our sins. Satan no longer has the right to hold onto the earth. But as long as the Jews do not accept Jesus and plead for His return, Jesus will not come again to the earth, and Satan can continue to rule the earth as if he had the right to do so. Knowing this, Satan will try every possible means to annihilate the Jews to make it sure that there are no Jews left to make the plea for His return.

If we know of Satan's scheme, we can understand why Israel had to suffer massacres throughout history, and why even today the Arab nations and their allies are trying to drive the Jews out of Palestine. The ultimate goal of Satanic power is to expunge the nation of Israel from the face of the earth. Should he be unable to achieve this goal for some reason, he at least wants to prevent Israel from occupying Palestine and existing as a nation. If the Jewish people do not exist as a nation, there is no chance that they can make a national repentance and national plea.

The reason why a national repentance and a national plea are required is that Israel's rejection of the Messiah was not a personal but a national sin committed by the leaders, who mislead the people. This is why the Arab nations did not and do not acknowledge Israel's independence of 1948, and are in battle with her for the purpose of obliterating her from the face of the earth. Of course, this would be their second choice next to the annihilation of all Jews.

Satan's plan of obliterating Israel from the face of the earth is not mere conjecture. The veracity of Satan's plan is plainly revealed in the Palestinian National Covenant. Article 15 of the Charter clearly states that the PLO aims at the "elimination of Zionism in Palestine." The correct translation of "elimination of Zionism" from Arabic is "liquidation of the Zionist presence—" and "the Zionist presence" is a common Arabic euphemism for the State of Israel. This euphemism may have been derived from the fact that the Zionist movement was formed initially to establish the state of Israel. So, this clause in fact calls for the destruction of the nation of Israel.

What is now going on in the Middle East, the fact that Israel is surrounded by the nations that aim at her destructtion, is fulfilling what is written in Psalm 83. The accuracy of the prophecy is remarkable and awesome. Moreover, the verse reading "They have said, 'Come, and let us cut them off from being a nation, that the name of Israel may be remembered no more" is exactly in accordance with the goal of the Palestinian National Covenant, "the destruction of the nation of Israel."

> Palms 83:
>
> Do not keep silent, O God! Do not hold your peace,
> And do not be still, O God!
>
> For behold, Your enemies make a tumult;
> And those who hate You have lifted up their head.
> They have taken crafty counsel against Your people.
>
> And consulted together against Your sheltered ones.
> They have said, **"Come, and let us cut them off**
> **From being a nation, that the name of**
> **Israel may be remembered no more."**
>
> For they have consulted together with one consent;
> They form a confederacy against You; the tents of
> Edom and the Ishmaelites; Moab and the Hagarites;
> Gebal, Ammon, and Amalek; Philistia with the
> inhabitants of Tyre; Assyria also has joined with
> them; They have helped the children of Lot. Selah

> Deal with them as with Midian, as with Sisera, as with Jabin at the Brook Kishon, who perished at En Dor, who became as refuse on the earth. Make their nobles like Oreb and like Zeeb, Yes, all their princes like Zebah and Zalmunna, who said, "Let us take for ourselves the pastures of God for a possession."
>
> O my God, make them like the whirling dust like the chaff before the wind! As the fire burns the woods, and as the flame sets the mountains on fire, so pursue them with Your tempest, and frighten them with Your storm.
>
> Fill their faces with shame, that they may seek your name, O Lord. Let them be confounded and dismayed forever; yes, let them be put to shame and perish, that men may know that You, whose name alone is the Lord, are the most High over all the earth.

Satan has deceived the church and the believers, but the works of Satan cannot be an excuse for our failure to arouse Israel to godly jealousy so that she may accept Jesus as her Messiah. The fact that God has allowed Satan to go at his full swing is what makes the period we live in, the Age of Grace, so meaningful.

The church is at present time operated in the realm of mystery. This is possible in this Age of Grace because the Father and the Son are dwelling in us through the Holy Spirit. So, we call this period prior to the Messianic Kingdom proper the 'Age of Mystery Kingdom of God.'

The grace we are receiving should be sufficient to overcome the wiles of Satan if we keep walking in the Spirit.

The burden lies on the saints that the church has not become an object of godly envy for emulation to the Jews but rather has become an object of their anger and derision.

The Church Age indeed will not come to an end unless the church completes its mission and Israel comes to accept Jesus as their Lord. Jesus then will return and establish the Kingdom of God on this earth.

VI.

The Full-Knowledge That Israel Needs to Know For Her Salvation

Prior to explaining God's plan for the salvation of Israel, Paul answered questions the Israelites harbored so that the plan will become more acceptable. First, the Jews wondered whether God's words failed because Israel failed. Secondly, they were skeptical concerning the salvation of the Gentiles. Paul answered these two questions in Romans 9:6-29, then elaborated on why Israel failed and what is required of Israel to obtain salvation in Romans 9:30-10:15.

Paul explained why God's word has not failed even if the nation of Israel had failed to attain the salvation. Paul deemed that the failure of Israel which is led by the unbelieving leaders should not be counted as failure of the fulfillment of God's word. He asserted that the fulfillment of the word of God is yet to come through the "remnants" of Israel. To make this point clear, Paul also explained who the 'remnants' of Israel are.

> But it is not that the word of God has taken no effect. For they are not all Israel who are of Israel nor are they all children because they are the seed of Abraham. But, "In Isaac your seed shall be called." That is, those who are the children of the flesh, these are

not the children of God; but the children of the promise are counted as the seed.

(Romans 9:6-8)

God promised to Abraham that He will bless all the families of the earth through him and his seed. For this purpose, he also gave Isaac out of the dead womb of Sarah.

What did God mean by the 'blessing' when He said in Genesis 12:2-3 that Abraham would be a 'blessing' and also in him all the families of the earth would be blessed? It was none other than the salvation of the world, the promise of the Kingdom of God on earth. In other words, God promised Abraham that He would save the world from its misery through the seed of Abraham.

Jesus Christ was the promised seed of Abraham. Isaac was the type of Jesus Christ, and was obedient to his father even to be offered as a sacrifice on the altar just as Jesus was obedient to His Father and bore the cross for the salvation of the world.

To point out the reason why the 'word of God' has not taken effect through the leaders at the time, Paul said, "They are not all Israel who are of Israel nor are they all children because they are the seed of Abraham." Paul meant that not all who are called by Israel are necessarily worthy of the name, Israel. The verse also underscored that not all the seeds of Abraham are 'the children.'

Paul then added to elaborate on 'the children,' "'In Isaac your seed shall be called.' That is, those who are the children of the flesh, these are not the children of God; but the children of the promise are counted as the seed."

To understand Paul's elaboration on 'the children,' it is essential to know what Paul meant by 'the children of the flesh' and 'the children of the promise' respectively. Paul gave a clue to these queries when he said in Galatians 4:28: "We (the Spirit-filled ones) are **the children of the promise as Isaac was.**" So, it is clear that Paul denoted the Spirit-filled believers by 'the children of the promise.' The reason that he called the Spirit-filled Christians 'the children of the promise' was that they received the eternal life of the Holy Spirit and will be resurrected from the dead according to God's promise to Jesus, just as Abraham received Isaac from the dead womb of Sarah according to God's promise. So he meant 'the children of God' by 'the children of the promise.'

Now it is not difficult to guess what 'the children of the flesh' means. They signify the men and women who are not born of the Spirit in contrast to the Spirit-filled 'children of the promise.' In other words, they are not 'the children of God.' One should not mistake the expression 'the children of the flesh' as all other descendants of Abraham than Isaac's. Even the descendants of Isaac can be 'the children of the flesh' if they are not born of the Spirit.

What Paul tried to say here was that the leaders who rejected Christ were not 'Israel' worthy of the name even if they were of Israel due to the fact that they were physically descendants of Isaac. They had no hope of receiving eternal life through Jesus Christ according to the promise of God because they had already rejected Him. In other words, God's word to Abraham is to be fulfilled in the future through the 'remnants' of Israel. They are the children of the promise, the Spirit-filled Messianic Jews.

For these reasons, the failure of Israel led by the leaders at the time cannot be counted as the failure of 'the word of God' to Abraham.

Paul, therefore, said as follows in Romans 9:27-29, quoting from Isaiah 10:22.

Isaiah also cries out concerning Israel:

> "Though the number of the children of Israel be as the sand of the sea, the remnant will be saved. For He will finish the work and cut it short in righteousness, because the Lord will make a short work upon the earth."

And as Isaiah said before:

> "Unless the Lord of Sabaoth had left us a seed,
> We would have become like Sodom, and we would have been made like Gomorrah.

> (Romans 9:27-29)

Then, Paul deals with the question on the salvation of Gentiles. He explains that Gentiles are also included among 'the vessels of mercy' that God has prepared for glory. To prove this, he quotes verses from Hosea in Romans 9:25-26:

> I will call them 'My people,' who were not My people, and her beloved who was not beloved,
> And it shall come to pass in the place where it was said to them, 'You are not My people,' there they will be called sons of the living God.

> (Romans 9:25-26)

These verses from Hosea are originally for Israel's restoration from her lost position, but Paul applied them to the conversion of Gentiles. Israel has long been bereaved of her right and position as the 'people of God' due to her sin of idolatry.

Paul also stated in Ephesians that God did not make known to man in earlier generations the details of the salvation of Gentiles, but He finally revealed to the apostles and prophets of Paul's generation that the Gentiles are also fellow heirs in Christ along with the Israelites:

> For this reason I, Paul, the prisoner of Christ Jesus for you Gentiles—if indeed you have heard of the dispensation of the grace of God which was given to me for you, how that by revelation He made known to me the mystery (as I wrote before in a few words, by which when you read, you may understand my knowledge in the mystery of Christ), which in other ages was not made known to the sons of men, as it has now been revealed by the Spirit to His holy apostles and prophets: that the Gentiles should be fellow heirs, of the same body, and partakers of His promise in heirs through the gospel, of which I became a minister according to the gift of the grace of God given to me by the effective working of His power.
>
> (Ephesians 3:1-7)

After answering the two questions that the Israelites harbored, Paul was now ready to explain why Israel as a nation had failed and what was required of Israel to obtain salvation in Romans 9:30-10:15:

What shall we say? That the Gentiles, who did not pursue righteousness, have attained to righteousness, even the righteousness of faith; but Israel, pursuing the law of righteousness has not attained to the law of righteousness. Why? Because they did not seek it by faith but as it were by the works of the law. For they stumbled over the stumbling stone. As it is written: "Behold, I lay in Zion a stumbling stone and rock of offence. And whoever believes on Him will not be put to shame."
Brothers, my heart's desire and prayer to God for Israel is that they may be saved. For I bear them witness that they have zeal for God, but not according to (full-)knowledge. For they being ignorant of God's righteousness, and seeking to establish their own righteousness, have not submitted to the righteousness of God. For Christ is the end of the law for righteousness to every one who believes.'

(Romans 9:30-10:4)

Paul ascribed the cause of Israel's failure to the lack of 'full-knowledge.' By 'full-knowledge' he meant the knowledge that one could obtain God's righteousness through believing in Jesus Christ rather than by trying to establish one's own righteousness by keeping the law. We must note that Paul used *epignosis* instead of *gnosis* in the Greek text. *Epignosis* denotes the "full-knowledge" while *gnosis* simply means the 'knowledge.'

The 'full-knowledge' is not the type of knowledge one can acquire through reasoning, but only through humility and a contrite heart. Everyone who repents and believes in

66

Christ will attain God's righteousness freely. It is possible because Christ died for us for the forgiveness of our sins so that whoever believes in Him might be reckoned as righteous as if the believer himself were crucified on the cross to pay back the price of his sin. This is the grace that God proffers freely upon everyone who comes into the world if he or she accepts it through His Son, Jesus Christ.

Paul then expounded further on God's righteousness, contrasting it with the righteousness of law by quoting Leviticus 18:5 and Deuteronomy 30:11-14:

> Moses writes about the righteousness which is of the law; "The man who does those things (laws) shall live by them." But the righteousness of faith speaks in this way, "Do not say in your heart, 'Who will ascend into heaven?' (that is, to bring Christ down from above) or 'Who will descend into the abyss?' (That is, to bring Christ up from the dead)." But what does it say? "The word is near you; even in your mouth and in your heart (that is, the word of faith which we preach)": that if you confess with your mouth, the Lord Jesus and believe in your heart that God has raised Him from the dead, you will be saved. For with the heart one believes to righteousness, and with the mouth confession is made to salvation. For the Scripture says, "Whoever believes on Him will not be put to shame."
>
> (Romans 10:5-11)

The verse, "The man who does these things shall live by them," is from Leviticus 18:5. This verse could have been applied under the Old Covenant because sins at that time could be covered temporarily with the blood of animals under the law until Christ came. This meant that the Old Testament saints were able to live by the righteousness of the law. But when Paul was writing this letter to the Romans, they were already under the New Covenant, and had no more valid sacrifice to offer for sins even if they had wanted to rely upon the law. Moreover, there was no reason for them anymore to live by the righteousness of the law which could only cover sins temporarily.

He explains how easy it is to be forgiven of sins and saved under the New Covenant. It is as simple as to believe in one's heart and to confess with one's mouth that Jesus is Lord. To be able to confess that Jesus is Lord with one's mouth is the proof that one has received the Holy Spirit because I Corinthians 12:3 says: "No one can say 'Jesus is Lord' except by the Holy Spirit." Accordingly, "with the mouth confession is made to salvation" as quoted above in fact means that one is saved by receiving the Holy Spirit. The full-knowledge that Israel needs to know to be saved is as easy as this.

Now, Paul wanted the Israelites to know that they need to hear the gospel of Jesus Christ again in order to be saved in the end days. Paul, who knew that the Gentiles would one day bring the gospel to Jerusalem, also wanted the Israelites to know that the Gentiles were called along with the Israelites to preach the gospel. So, he prepared them with these words in Romans 10:12-15:

> For there is no distinction between Jew and Greek, for the same Lord over all is rich to all who call upon Him, for "whoever calls upon the name of the Lord shall be saved." How then shall they call on Him in

whom they have not believed? And how shall they believe in Him of whom they have not heard? And how shall they hear without a preacher? And how shall they preach unless they are sent? As it is written:

"How beautiful are the feet of those who preach the gospel of peace, who bring glad tidings of good things!"

(Romans 10:12-15)

Paul also confirmed the verse in Isaiah 52:7 which he quoted here is about the Gentile nation that will bring the gospel to Jerusalem.

VII. 

A Gentile Nation That Will Arouse Israel to Godly Jealousy

Israel's contemporary state at the time of Paul was in accordance with what had been said by Isaiah in his prophecy. Israel heard the gospel, but not believed it. Paul confirms this in Romans 10:16-18.

> But they have not all (as a whole nation) obeyed the gospel. For Isaiah says, "Lord, who has believed our report?" So then faith comes by hearing, and hearing by the word of God. But I say, have they not heard? Yes indeed, "Their sound has gone out to the end of the entire land of God.[3]

> (Romans 10:16-18)

Israel, as a nation could not attain salvation because the leaders who represented Israel did not accept the gospel of Jesus Christ. Only a handful of people accepted it. The

---

[3] Paul used Greek word *oikoumenei* to translate the Hebrew word *tebel* when he quoted Psalm 19:4 here. *Oikoumenei* means the land where Greeks rather than barbarians live. Paul must have thought *oikoumenei* the right word for *tebel* because *tebel* also means a land where a special people live, that is, where the people of God live, the land of Israel. It is a mistake if one translates *oikoumenei* into "earth" as if it were *gei* which means "the earth" in Greek.

disappointed ones were not the leaders and their followers but the remnants who believed in Jesus Christ.

The leaders could take the fact that Israel had not been saved as proof that Jesus was not the Messiah. But the believers in Christ could not understand how Israel was left out of the salvation. They were dismayed and confused by what had happened.

Paul addresses himself to this confused and bewildered group of Israelites by quoting verses from Deuteronomy 32:21b and Isaiah 65:1a & 2a in Romans 10:19-21:

> But I say, did Israel not know? First Moses says:
> "I will provoke you to jealousy by those
> Who are not My people,[4]

---

[4] This important phrase is often misinterpreted, and the cause of it is in the translation of the Hebrew words '*lo am.*' '*Lo*' means 'no' and '*am*' is 'people'; so its literal translation would be 'no people' or 'no nation.' But *Gesenius' Hebrew-Chaldee Lexicon* (Tregelles 1980) says that '*am*' is very often used of Israel, as being the 'people of God.' Therefore '*am*' denotes 'God's people', and '*lo am*' should rightly be translated to mean 'not God's people,' which is a 'Gentile people' or a 'Gentile nation' instead of "no people" or "no nation."

However, most English versions of the New Testament translated it as "no nation," "not a people" or "not a nation." For this reason, readers of such translations had difficulty in understanding it as "a Gentile people" or "a Gentile nation."

Some commentary even suggests it to be "the church," but it cannot denote "the church" because Isaiah 65:1 qualifies this nation to be a nation that never sought God or called on His name before she was called by God. But the

I will anger you by a foolish nation. (Deut. 32:21)"

But Isaiah is very bold and says:

"I was found by those who did not seek Me;
I was made manifest to those
Who did not ask for Me (Is. 65:1a)."
("I said, 'Here I am, here I am,' to a nation
Which did not call on My name (Is.65:1b).")[5]

But to Israel he says

"All day long I have stretched out My hands
To a disobedient and contrary people (Is. 65:2)."
(Romans 10:19-21)

Despite Israel's offence of rejecting Christ, Paul asserted that God was not finished with Israel yet because God had another plan for Israel's salvation. To explain this, Paul quoted Deuteronomy 32:21b and Isaiah 65:1a & 2a from the books of Moses and Isaiah. He said that God was going to arouse Israel to godly jealousy by those who were 'not My people'—that is, a 'Gentile nation.' The reason for His doing this was because Israel first provoked God to jealousy with idols that were not God.

Then Paul qualified the Gentile nation by quoting Isaiah 65:1a in Romans 10:20, which said that God was found by

---

church has been, from its inception, composed of the believers who had already called on His name.

[5] This verse is in Isaiah 65:1b, but not quoted by Paul in the Romans. He quoted only Is. 65:1a & 2a, the first parts of Is. 65:1 & 2, instead of the whole verses. He seemed to have done this to make the quotation as little as possible so that he could probably spare the limited space.

a Gentile nation which had never sought or asked for Him.

Indeed, the Lord was found by a nation about 220 years ago when a group of scholars in Seoul got interested in a book on Catholic doctrine that accidentally flowed into the group along with other books they ordered from Beijing. The Catholic catechism, to those who had never heard about such a thing before, was a mystery in and of itself. The group, however, studied the doctrine and discussed about it among themselves for about 150 years before they finally decided to send an envoy to Beijing to find out what it was about.

The envoy, by the name of Sweng-hoon Lee, was the first known Korean to be baptized. His baptism took place at a catholic church in Beijing in A.D. 1784. This was about 150 years after the group received the first book on Catholic doctrine. During his several-month stay in Beijing, he was baptized and tried his best to learn as much about Catholicism as possible. Upon his return to Seoul, he became the first lay leader and began to teach and baptize his colleagues. They built churches in Seoul and the nearby countryside all by themselves, without any help from clergymen or missionaries. They had to do this because there were no clergymen or missionaries available until 1794. (These historical facts are from '*The History of Protestant Missions in Korea 1832-1910,*' by Paik, Lak-Geoon George.)

Before they came to know the mysterious and uncanny book of Catholic doctrine, no one in the nation sought or asked for the Lord. This is how the verse from Isaiah 65:1a, "I was found by those who did not seek Me; I was made manifest to those who did not ask for Him" has come to be realized.

Indeed, this was a nation that He called saying, "Here I am, here I am." The way Christianity was introduced into Korea was unique in that no missionary had been sent to her to preach the gospel before they came to know the Lord. Instead, Koreans themselves sent an envoy to find the Lord, so that the Lord might be found in the way that was prophesied in Isaiah 65:1b. The Lord was merely calling them, saying, "Here I am, here I am." The fact that the book on Catholic doctrine flowed into the hands of the scholars was not an accident, but it must have been His way of saying "Here I am, here I am."

It was God's plan to stir up one nation from among the Gentiles and make it His and make that nation shoulder the mission to arouse Israel to godly envy for emulation on behalf of the church. God will have that nation carry out this mission—to teach the world about God's mercy, justice, and the gospel of salvation, a mission that was supposedly Israel's. As a result, Korea will make Israel envious so that she will return to Christ Jesus.

We know the story of unbelieving Thomas, one of the twelve Disciples of Christ. Thomas heard the news that Christ was raised after His death on the cross, but he did not believe. Jesus later appeared before him again and gently pulled his hand to the wound on his side and made him feel it, and then Thomas believed. God's plan for Israel's salvation is somewhat similar to what He did for Thomas.

In like manner, God has a plan for the unbelieving Israel. He will stir up a Gentile nation in which the gospel is realized so that Israel can see, touch, and feel it, and turn to Christ out of envy.

Isaiah tried to delineate the character of this particular nation in Isaiah 41:25-27, 52:7, 55:1-13 and 65:1. Note that all of these verses are in the latter part of the book of Isaiah, that is, in chapters 40-66.

In Isaiah 41:25-27, Isaiah described the character of that nation for the first time as follows:

> I have raised up one from the north, and he shall come; from the rising of the sun (east) he shall call on My name; and he shall come against the princes as though mortar, as the potter treads clay.

> Who told of this from the beginning, so we could know, or beforehand, so we could say, 'He was right'? No one told of this, no one foretold it, no one heard any word from you (the idols). [*Verse 26 is from NIV]

> The first time I said to Zion, "Look, there they are! And I will give to Jerusalem one who brings good tidings.

> (Isaiah 41:25-27)

These verses are often misconstrued as words that describe Cyrus of Persia because these verses are also in chapter 41 following the description of Cyrus. But the story of Cyrus is in the first part of the chapter which comprises verses 1-16, while these verses are in the second part of the chapter which comprises verses 17-29. The second part of chapter 41 introduces another Gentile nation that is called by God for Israel's ultimate salvation.

As a matter of fact, chapters 40-66, the latter part of the book of Isaiah, deals with two themes, namely 'Israel's deliverance from Babylonian Captivity' and 'the ultimate salvation of Israel' that will result in the salvation of the world at the end. One of the reasons that God presented these two themes in the latter part of Isaiah was to make Israel believe on their ultimate salvation after experiencing the faithfulness of God who delivered Israel from Babylon as He spoke in the book of Isaiah.

So God expected Israel to say, "He was right!" after being delivered from Babylon. God also expected that Israel would consider the 'former things,' the deliverance from Babylon and come to know the latter end of them, which is their ultimate salvation as explained in the book of Isaiah. In other words, God anticipated that Israelites would believe that faithful God will keep His words spoken through the prophet Isaiah by delivering Israel again from their hopeless life of Diaspora in the latter days.

Isaiah explained how God will use Cyrus of Persia to deliver Israel from Babylon in the first part of chapter 41, then he described in the second part of the chapter, another Gentile nation that God called to assist Israel's ultimate salvation along with the salvation of the entire world.

The second part of Isaiah 41 begins in verse 17 with these words. "When the poor and needy seek water, and there is none, and their tongues fail for thirst, I, the Lord, will hear them; I, the God of Israel, will not forsake them." These verses aptly describe Israel's dire need for her salvation. Isaiah used an expression 'the poor and needy' for the 'remnants' of Israel who sought Israel's salvation. Then in verses 18-20, he described the blessing of God in the Kingdom when they are saved from the affliction of the thirst described in verse 17 as follows:

> I will open rivers in desolate heights, and fountains in the midst of the valleys; I will make the wilderness a pool of water, and the dry land springs of water. I will plant in the wilderness the cedar and the acacia tree, the myrtle and the oil tree; I will set in the desert the cypress tree and the pine and the box tree together, that they may see and know, and consider and understand together, that the hand of the Lord has done this, and the Holy One of Israel has created it.

> (Isaiah 41:17-20)

These are descriptions of the blessing of the Kingdom of God on earth. This is what God is going to do on this earth for Israelites and the people of the world.

Then in verses 21-24, Isaiah described how God taunted idols for their ignorance about the things to come:

> "Present your case," says the Lord. "Bring forth your strong reasons," says the King of Jacob. "Let them bring forth and show us what will happen; let them show the former things (the Babylonian Captivity), what they are that we may consider them, and know the latter end of them (the ultimate salvation of Israel); or declare to us things to come. Show the things that are to come hereafter, that we may know that you are gods; yes, do good or do evil, that we

may be dismayed and see it together. Indeed you are nothing, and your work is nothing; he who chooses you is an abomination.

(Is. 41:21-24)

Now, God finally tells about the nation that He will raise up for Israel's salvation in verses 25-27, as follows:

I have raised up one from the north, and he shall come from the rising of the sun (east) he shall call on My name; and he shall come against the princes as though mortar, as the potter treads clay.

Who told of this from the beginning, so we could know, or beforehand, so we could say, 'He was right'? No one told of this, no one foretold it, no one heard any word from you (the idols). (*Verse 26 is from NIV)

The first time I said to Zion, "Look, there they are! And I will give to Jerusalem one who brings good tidings.

(Isaiah 41:25-27)

As it was mentioned above, chapter 41 of Isaiah described two characters that came to help the afflicted Israel for the sake of Yahweh. One was Cyrus of Persia, and the other one was the one stirred up from the north and coming from the east.

It is important to note that the one God will stirred up from the north is a different person from Cyrus of Persia. One of the two reasons that he is different from Cyrus is that he should be a believer of Yahweh because Isaiah 41:25 says, "he shall call on 'My name,'" while Cyrus was not a believer. Moreover, 41:27 says that he is the one to

79

bring good tidings to Jerusalem, but God spoke of Cyrus in Isaiah 45:4, "For Jacob My servant's sake, and Israel My elect, I have even called you by your name; I have named you, though you have not known Me. I am the Lord, and there is no other; there is no God besides Me."

Also, Cyrus himself did not call Yahweh by 'my God' but 'his God' instead, when he made a proclamation throughout his kingdom as follows:

> Thus says Cyrus king of Persia: All the kingdoms of the earth the Lord God of heaven has given me. And He has commanded me to build Him a house at Jerusalem which is in Judah.

> Who is there among you of all His people? May 'his God' be with him! Now let him go up to Jerusalem, which is in Judah, and build the house of the Lord God of Israel (He is God), which is in Jerusalem.

> (Ezra 1:2-4)

The second reason why he is not the same person as Cyrus is that Cyrus was not stirred up from the north but from the east as Isaiah 41:2 clearly states, "Who raised up one from the east?" (The Hebrew word 'haair' was translated as 'raise up' in NKJV, as 'stir up' in NIV and as 'arouse' in NASB respectively.)

God wanted to show Israel and have her touch and feel the nation that she could have been, so that Israel, which did not believe upon merely hearing, would be able to believe.

As the Lord called Cyrus of Persia to deliver Israel from the Babylonian Captivity, so is God raising up a Gentile nation in the latter days to save His servant, Israel. Israel will return to Christ only when she sees with her eyes, touches with her hands and feels a nation that has become righteous, rich, and powerful by virtue of believing in Christ and has come to lead the nations with God's justice.

So far, Israel has not seen any Christian nation or even the church that practices God's justice and mercy to their satisfaction or what they think the Messiah might do. Israel needs to see and touch to feel a nation that has become a nation of justice and power through God's grace. To show such a nation to His servant Israel, God is preparing a Gentile nation.

As we learned in Romans 10:19-21, Paul first mentioned the Gentile nation by which God was going to make Israel jealous by quoting Deuteronomy 32:21b, and he qualified the nation as being a nation that had never sought or called on God's name by quoting Isaiah 65:1a. Then he also spoke of the disobedient Israel, which God was waiting to return to Him, by quoting Isaiah 65:2a.

In fact, the short verses from Deuteronomy and Isaiah mentioned here are all that Paul quoted to explain God's plan for the salvation of Israel. Paul, of course, never expected that the readers of his epistle to the Romans would be able to fully grasp God's plan for the salvation of Israel with these short quotations from Deuteronomy and Isaiah alone.

He knew that these were merely glimpses of what was contained in the books of Moses and Isaiah, and would remind readers that God had already revealed His plan in those books. Paul also knew that it takes knowledge of the whole Scripture, or at least knowledge of chapters 40-66 of

Isaiah—the latter part of Isaiah—and chapter 32 of Deuteronomy, to fully understand God's plan for the salvation of Israel. However, we can see Paul's wisdom in his quoting Deuteronomy 32:21b and Isaiah 65:1a & 2a in the book of Romans to explain God's plan for Israel's salvation.

It was of course necessary for Paul to quote Deuteronomy 32:21b in Romans to introduce the Gentile nation. But why did he quote Isaiah 65:1a & 2a out of so many verses in the book of Isaiah? Paul obviously wanted the readers of Romans to pay attention to chapter 65 of Isaiah and come to know thoroughly of its contents and its importance.

Paul wanted his readers to know this chapter thoroughly because chapter 65 was the summary and conclusion of the latter part of Isaiah, where God's plan for Israel's salvation was described. Hence, chapter 65 is in fact the summary of God's plan for Israel's salvation, and it tells us the three most important themes for Israel's salvation: first, the 'Gentile nation' that will arouse Israel to godly jealousy; second, the 'remnants' of Israel, who will fulfill the words of God; and third, the 'Kingdom of God' on earth that is to come when Israel returns to Christ.

In fact, verse 1 of Isaiah 65—in addition to Isaiah 41:25-27, 52:7, 55:1-13—explained more about the character of the 'Gentile nation' that will be used of God for Israel's salvation. The verse that tells the way in which the nation will come to know the Lord, is of a great help in identifying the Gentile nation.

In Isaiah 65:2-16 following the first verse, Isaiah contrasted the Gentile nation with disobedient Israel. He also explained in this section the emerging of the 'remnants' of Israel in detail.

Then he finished the chapter by describing the Kingdom of God to come when Israel returned to Christ in verses 17-25.

Paul ingeniously summarized these three themes from Isaiah 65 in Romans 10:20-11:15, and achieved the goal of informing the readers about the gist of God's plan for Israel's salvation, which was described in the latter part of Isaiah—chapters 40-66.

Moreover, Isaiah chapter 65 is God's response to the penitent prayer offered by the leaders of Israel that is described in Isaiah 63:7-64:12. The leaders of Israel indeed will have to repent for not having accepted Jesus as it was predicted in Hosea 5:15. The penitent prayer ends as follows:

> Will you restrain Yourself because of these things,
> O Lord? Will you hold your peace, and afflict us
> very severely?
>
> (Isaiah 64:12)

God's answer to their prayer begins also in chapter 65 with a notion that He neither held His peace, nor will He hold His peace in the future. He said in the first verse as follows:

> I was sought by those who did not ask for Me;
> I was found by those who did not seek Me,
> I said, "Here I am, here I am," to a nation
> Which did not call on My name.
>
> (Isaiah 65:1)

Isaiah 65:1a is the verse that is quoted in Romans 10:20. The fact that God did not hold His peace is evident because He had called Gentile nation that did not seek Him, ask for Him, or call on His name in preparation for Israel's salvation. God has not been holding His peace but has been beckoning toward that Gentile nation, calling "Here I am, here I am," so that this nation may come to know Him, live according to the gospel, and spread God's love and justice throughout the world.

On the other hand, Isaiah 65:2, says that God has not held His peace but has been stretching His hands out all day long to a rebellious people who live according to their own thoughts, calling them to return to Him as follows:

> I have stretched out My hands all day long
>> To a rebellious people,
> Who walk in a way that is not good,
>> According to their own thoughts
>>>> (Isaiah 65:2)

Then Isaiah continues to say that He will not hold His peace, even in the future, because He will continue to stretch out His hands to call the disobedient people to return to be culled as the 'remnants' as follows:

> A people who provoke Me to anger
>> Continually to My face;
> Who sacrifice in gardens,
>> And burn incense on altars of brick;
> Who sit among the graves,
>> And spend the night in the tombs;
> Who eat swine's flesh,
>> And the broth of abominable things

Is in their Vessels
Who say, "Keep to yourself, do not come near me,
 For I am holier than you."
These are smoke in My nostrils,
 A fire that burns all the day.

Behold, it is written before Me;
 I will not keep silence, but will repay—
 Even repay into their bosom—
 Your iniquities and the iniquities of your
 Fathers together," says the Lord.

Who have burned incense on the mountains
 And blasphemed Me on the hills;
Therefore I will measure their former work
 Into their bosom

Thus says the Lord:
As the new wine is found in the cluster, and one
 Says, 'Do not destroy it, for a blessing is in it.'
So will I do for My servants' sake
 That I may not destroy them all
 I will bring forth descendants from Jacob.
 And from Judah an heir of My Mountains
 My elect shall inherit it, and My servants
 Shall dwell there.

Sharon shall be a fold of flocks,
 And the Valley of Achor, a place of herds
 To lie down, for My people who have sought Me.
But you are those who forsake the Lord, who forget
 My holy mountain

(Isaiah 65:3-16)

85

In this manner, God is calling and waiting for those select persons in Israel who are obedient and good enough to produce new wine. These are the 'remnants' that will be saved.

But Paul had to condense these from Isaiah 65:2-16 and add in the beginning of Romans chapter 11 after quoting Isaiah 65:1 at the end of Romans chapter 10, as follows:

> I say then, has God cast away His people? Certainly not! I also am an Israelite, of the seed of Abraham, of the tribe of Benjamin. God has not cast away His people whom He foreknew. Or do you not know what the Scripture says of Elijah, how he pleads with God against Israel saying, 'Lord, they have killed your prophets and torn down Your altars, and I alone am left, and they seek my life.' But what does the divine response say to him? 'I have reserved for Myself seven thousand men who have not bowed the knee to Baal.' Even so then, at this present time there is a remnant according to the election of grace. And if by grace then it is no longer of works; otherwise grace is no longer grace. But if it is of works, it is no longer grace; otherwise work is no longer work. What then? Israel has not obtained what it seeks; but the elect (one who chose the grace of God) obtained it, and the rest were hardened.

> Just as it is written:

> God has given them a Spirit of Stupor,
> Eyes that they should not see
> And ears that they should not hear,
> To this very day.

> And David says:

Let their table become a snare and a trap,
A stumbling block and recompense to them;
Let their eyes be darkened, that they may not see,
And bow down their back always.

(Romans 11:1-10)

Isaiah now, after elaborating on the 'Gentile nation' and 'the remnant of Israel' finished chapter 65 with a description of the 'Kingdom of God' to come.

The rest of Isaiah chapter 65—verses 17-25—describes a new heaven and a new earth, the millennial blessing that will come when Israel accepts Jesus as her Messiah. He began it with these words:

> For behold, I create new heavens and a new earth;
> And the former shall not be remembered
> Or come to mind.

> But be glad and rejoice forever in what I create;
> For behold, I create Jerusalem as a rejoicing,
> And her people a joy

> I will rejoice in Jerusalem, and joy in My people;
> The voice of weeping shall no longer be heard in her,
> Nor the voice of crying.

> No more shall an infant from there live but a few days,
> Nor an old man who has not fulfilled his days;
> For the child shall die one hundred years old,
> But the sinners being one hundred years old
> Be accursed.

> They shall build houses and inhabit them;
> They shall plant vineyards and eat their fruit.
> They shall not build and another inhabit;

87

They shall not plant and another eats;
For as the days of a tree,
So shall be the days of My people,

And my elect shall long enjoy the work of their hands
They shall not labor in vain,
Nor bring forth children for trouble;
For they shall be the descendants of the blessed of
The Lord, and their offspring with them.
It shall come to pass that before they call, I will answer,
And while they are still speaking, I will hear.

The wolf and the lamb shall feed together,
The lion shall eat straw like ox,
And dust shall be the serpent's food.
They shall not hurt nor destroy
In all My holy mountain, says the Lord.

(Isaiah 65:17-25)

Paul again condensed this portion of Isaiah Chapter 65 in Romans 11:11-15 as follows:

I say then, have they stumbled that they should fall? Certainly not! But through their fall, to provoke them to godly jealousy, salvation has come to the Gentiles. Now if their fall is riches for the world, and their failure riches for the Gentiles, how much more their fullness! For I speak to you Gentiles; inasmuch as I am an apostle to the Gentiles, I magnify my ministry, if by any means I may provoke to godly jealousy those who are my flesh and save some of them [the "remnants"]. For if their being cast away is the reconciling of the world, what will their acceptance be but life from the dead?

(Romans 11:11-15).

Paul used the powerful four words **'life from the dead'** to signify the enormous blessing of the Millennial Kingdom. The new life in the coming age is the glory of God's presence itself and certainly will remove most of the curses placed on the earth for the restoration of all creatures.

He also explains that this blessing will not come until Israel accepts Jesus Christ, and goes on to announce his central message to the Gentile believers to have those who are his flesh (the Jews) aroused to godly jealousy so that the 'remnants' of Israel may also be saved to restore the nation of Israel to fulfill the Words of God.

Per the explanation thus far, it is clear what God is trying to convey to us in Romans 10:19-11:15. It is essentially the condensation of Isaiah chapter 65 which is the summery of God's plan of the salvation of Israel described in the latter part of Isaiah chapters 40-66.

As pointed out previously, Isaiah chapter 65 is also God's reply to the penitent prayer offered by the leaders of the Jewish people during the tribulation. His reply to them was an offer of the Kingdom of God on earth where their sufferings will be removed and tears wiped out from their eyes. What can be a reply that will satisfy them more? God has promised to deliver them from all of their sufferings and lead them to have the eternal life in the Kingdom on earth. This surely confirms the loving kindness of our Lord, God.

God is now at work to raise up a Gentile nation and sanctify her—having cleansed her with the Word—to be a nation that embraces the gospel of Christ, God's love, and His justice. In this way, Israel, which did not believe, will see and touch to feel this nation and be moved to godly jealousy so that she may return to Christ Jesus.

God's plan to save Israel through a Gentile nation is made more certain by Isaiah 55:1-13, which reveals the nation that Israel will call on to hear God's message.

These verses are essentially recapitulation of Isaiah 41:25-27, that we perused previously:

Isaiah: 55:1-13:

> 1-4   Ho! Everyone who thirsts, come to the waters; and you who have no money, come, buy and eat! Yes, come, buy wine and milk without money and without price. Why do you spend money for what is not bread, and your wages for what does not satisfy? Listen diligently to Me and eat what is good, and let your soul delight itself in abundance. Incline your ear, and Come to Me. Hear, and your soul shall live; and I will make an everlasting covenant with you—the sure mercies of David. Indeed I have given Him as a witness to the people, a leader and commander for the people.
>
> (Isaiah: 55:1–4)

God pleads with Israelites not to waste money on what is neither satisfying nor good for their soul, but listen to Him and eat what is good so that their souls may live and delight themselves in abundance of the Kingdom of God. For this,

He also said, "Incline your ear, and come to Me. Hear and your soul shall live; and I will make an everlasting covenant with you—the sure mercies of David."

What God meant by 'the sure mercies of David' is 'the promise that God made with David that He will give the Messiah among his descendants out of His faithful mercies for David. This is the promise that God made with David as it is described in II Samuel 7:4-17, and is called 'Davidic Covenant.'

The Messiah from the seed of David is a witness of the Father to the people for His love, also is a leader and commander for the people. He will die on the cross to witness the Father's love for the people so that everyone who believes in Him may receive the everlasting life.

Then, He continues to tell about the nation that will bring them the good news which will enable them to receive the everlasting life.

> 5-7   Surely you shall call a nation you do not know, and they[6] that do not know you shall run to you, because of the Lord your God, the Holy One of Israel, for he has glorified you.

---

[6] 'They' was merely inserted here in translation as the subject of the 3rd person plural form of the verb 'rutzu (run).' 'They,' therefore, refers to the people of the nation when Isaiah said in verse 5, "Surely you shall call a nation you do not know, and <u>they</u> (the people of the nation) that do not know you shall run to you, because of the Lord your God, the Holy One of Israel, for He has glorified you." But, the major English versions such as KJ, NIV, NASB erroneously used 'nations' or 'nation' in place of 'they'.

Seek the Lord while He may be found, call upon Him while he is near. Let the wicked forsake his way, and the unrighteous man his thoughts; let him return to the Lord, and He will have mercy on him, and to our God, for He will abundantly pardon.

Israel will call to the Gentile nation that God prepared for Israel, and that nation will rush to Israel for the sake of Yahweh their God to preach the gospel of Jesus Christ among them.

The primary nation, however, chosen by God for Israel in the end days is not a number of nations, but one nation. It is clear that the burden for the mission lies on us all—the entire church. But it is not unusual that God chooses certain nation or people for a particular task. In fact, God does His work more in this manner than by assigning the task to all the saints of the church, even though He expects the prayers and supports from all saints. It is, for example, much the same way that God chose the United States as the primary nation to send missionaries to the Korean peninsula more than 120 years ago.

In verses 6 and 7, God pleads with Israel to seek Yahweh while He is near and can be found. "Seek the Lord while He may be found; call on Him while he is near. Let the wicked forsake his way and the evil man his thoughts. Let him turn to the Lord, and He will have mercy on him, and our God, for he will freely pardon."

God was concerned that the Israelites, because of their pride as the chosen people of God, might spurn the gospel or the people who bring the good news to them. So, He added verses 8-13. He began this portion with the words,

"For My thoughts are not your thoughts, neither are your ways My ways, declares the Lord."

God knew that the Israelites would not be very happy to hear the good news of their God from the Gentiles. In fact, Israel knew that they were supposed to be teaching the Gentiles. Israel was not happy when God said that He was going to deliver them from Babylon through Cyrus of Persia, either. Then, God said to Israel:

> Woe to him who strives with his Maker! Let the potsherd strive with the potsherds of the earth! Shall the clay say to him who forms it, "What are you making?" Or shall your handiwork say, "He has no hands"? Woe to him who says to his father "What are you begetting?" Or to the woman, "What have you brought forth?"
>
> Thus says the Lord, the Holy One of Israel, and his Maker: "Ask Me of things to come concerning My sons? And concerning the work of My hands, you command Me? I have made the earth, and created man on it. It was I—My hands that stretched out the heavens, and all their host I have commanded. I have raised him (Cyrus) up in righteousness, and I will direct all his ways; he shall build My city and let My exiles go free, not for price nor reward, says the Lord of hosts.
>
> (Isaiah 45:9-13)

God plainly tells Israel that His plan is once again to use a Gentile nation for Israel's salvation as He used Cyrus of Persia to deliver them from the Babylonian Captivity. Then He continues to plead with Israelites in these words:

8-13   For My thoughts are not your thoughts, nor are your ways My ways, says the Lord. For as the heavens are higher than the earth, so are My ways higher than your ways and so are My thoughts than your thoughts. For as the rain comes down, and the snow from heaven, and do not return there, but water the earth and make it bring forth and bud, that it may give seed to the sower and bread to the eater, so shall My word be that goes forth from My mouth; it shall not return to Me void, but it shall accomplish what I please, and it shall prosper in the thing for which I sent it.

For you shall go out with joy, and be led out with peace; the mountains and the hills shall break forth into singing before you, and all the trees of the field shall clap their hands. Instead of the thorn shall come up the cypress tree, and instead of the brier shall come up the myrtle tree; and it shall be to the Lord for a name, for an everlasting sign that shall not be cut off.

(Isaiah 55:8–13)

Since the Lord said that what goes forth from His mouth will not return to Him void, why do we doubt? It is assured that the Church Age will not come to an end until the church completes her mission of arousing Israel to godly jealousy for emulation!

In Closing,

The unification of Korea will therefore mark the beginning of the 'unified stage of the fourth kingdom' before entering into the 'ten kingdom stage' which is described in the book of Daniel.

From then on, the Gentile nation will rapidly begin to shape up to become a nation that will move Israel to godly jealousy. God will pour out the Spirit of renewal on the nation to an extent that the church has never experienced such in its history except probably in the era of the early church.

During this period, not only the church of the Gentile nation but also of the whole world will prepare for the harvest time. As Jesus explained in Matthew chapter 13, the reapers will gather tares and bind them in bundles to be burned in fire but the righteous will shine forth as the sun in the kingdom of their Father. This period will indeed be the time in which the 'Axis of God' will be consolidated, and grow to befit the name and the task ahead.

The 'Axis of God' may be centered somewhere in the Northeast Asian bloc of the future ten kingdoms. It is reasonable to suppose that the military power of the Northeast Asian alliance may then be the sole power which can harass Antichrist's army as Daniel 11:44-45 says, "But news from the east and the north shall trouble him (Antichrist); therefore he shall go out with great fury to destroy and annihilate many. And he shall plant the tents of his palace between the seas and the glorious holy mountain; yet he shall come to his end, and no one will help him (Dan. 11:44-45)."

The northeastern expanse of Asia in which the Goguryeo Dynasty of Korea once thrived may be the crucial geopolitical spot in the struggle between 'the Axis of Evil' and the 'Axis of God.' before the wrath of Armageddon. There was a reason why Red China under Jiang Zemin about four years ago in 2002 began what was known as Beijing University's 'Northeast Asian History Project' in which China claimed a far fetched theory that the Goguryeo Dynasty of Korea was a part of China's provincial government. Needless to say, the claim was fabricated for a political purpose.

As the super power of the world and an ally of the Republic of Korea, America should not allow North Korea to fall under the Chinese hand when Kim Jong-il falls apart lest the Chinese plot may succeed. America instead, should by all means side with Korea when she comes to claim the expanse where the Goguryeo Dynasty thrived belongs to the Republic of Korea. This is not only for Korea but also for the sake of the task that the 'Axis of God' will have to carry out in the future.

The ten kingdom stage of the fourth empire in the age of Gentiles is unique in the way that has been symbolized by ten toes and the toes are not made of iron only but mingled with ceramic clay in the book of Daniel.

The head of the image in the dream of King Nebuchadnezzar was made of fine gold, its chest and arms of silver, its belly and thighs of bronze, its legs which represented the fourth kingdom was supposed to be of iron. But the ceramic clay was introduced in the feet of the fourth kingdom, to divide the kingdom as Daniel 2:41 says, "Whereas you saw the feet and toes, partly of potter's clay and partly of iron, the kingdom shall be divided; yet the strength of the iron shall be in it, just as you saw the iron mixed with ceramic clay."

If gold, silver, bronze, iron are the symbolic metals for the four beasts of the Gentile empires, ceramic clay can be something foreign to those beastly Gentiles.

The mingling with the clay in fact begins at the feet stage in Daniel 2:41, but the effect of the mingling appears only on ten kingdom stage of ten toes according to v. 42, with a notion that a relatively long period of time has passed since the introduction of ceramic clay into the feet. Daniel 2:40-43 described the event as follows:

> 40 And the fourth kingdom shall be as strong as iron, inasmuch as iron breaks in pieces and shatters all things; and like iron that crushes, that kingdom will break in pieces and crush all the others.

> 41 Whereas you saw the <u>feet</u> and toes, partly of potter's clay and partly of iron, the kingdom shall be divided; yet the strength of the iron shall be in it, just as you saw the iron mixed with ceramic clay.

> 42 And as the toes of the feet were partly of iron and partly of clay, so the kingdom shall be partly strong and partly fragile.

43   As you saw iron mixed with ceramic clay, they will mingle with the seed of men; but they will not adhere to one another, just as iron does not mix with clay.

(Daniel 2:40-42)

We can tell from v. 41 that the intention of introducing the ceramic clay to the feet and the toes of the kingdom is to change the strong and destructive character of the kingdom into a character which opposes it. The character of the fourth kingdom is said to be as strong as iron, and crushes all things in pieces, but the ceramic clay should oppose the character because the ceramic clay is said to be fragile. The people cannot remain united and divided in the kingdom as iron does not mix with clay. Nevertheless, it is also said that the fourth kingdom will keep its strong and destructive character in it despite the fact that the opposing character of ceramic clay are introduced. We can probably assume that the ceramic clay may be of God because it opposes the destructive beastly character of iron.

What then will ceramic clay symbolize, and why Daniel tried to clarify the fact that ceramic clay entered in the time of feet before its effects fully appear in the divided ten kingdoms stage as it is said in v. 42, "the toes of the feet were partly of iron and partly of clay, so the kingdom shall be partly strong and partly fragile."

Many expositors guess that the ceramic clay represents the democratic form of government in contrast to the iron which represents the totalitarian form of government. Since the ceramic clay is introduced to oppose the destructive character of the iron, it is reasonable to think that the ceramic clay symbolizes the democratic form of government which opposes the destructive character of the totalitarian form of governments.

Though reasonable may it appear to suppose that the ceramic clay represents the democratic form of governments, not all the governments that claim to be democratic belong to the ceramic clay type of nation because, for instance, Red China, and North Korea claim their governments to be democratic and bear the name such as 'the People's Democratic Republic.' Not only that, Great Britain today is counted as a birth place of western democracy and one of the most exemplary democratic nations in the world but she is a nation that still call her citizens by 'King's subjects' Therefore, we need to qualify the 'democratic form of governments' which are represented by the ceramic clay to distinguish these from them.

In 2004 at the Republican Convention, the vice president of the United States Dick Cheney quoted what the historian Bernard DeVoto once wrote. He said that when America was created the stars must have danced in the sky. The stars in the sky were indeed glad because God sowed the very seed of the ceramic clay type of democracy then in 1776, and was waiting to see it bear fruits in due time. The ceramic clay type of democracy most likely represents the democracy that is based on the human rights which stem from the premise that 'all men are created equal.' God must be very pleased to see that it has already budded, bloomed and begun to bear fruits first in American soil, and then spread all around the world. The fruits are expected to appear fully mature by the time when His servants take on the power of Antichrist, the "Axis of Evil."

The seed of the ceramic clay type of democracy was sown by God in the land of the new nation, the United States of America way before the time of ten kingdoms. This was why Daniel tried to clarify in Daniel 2:41-42 that there was a fairly long period of time gap between the time that ceramic clay was introduced in the feet stage and the time that its effects would appear fully in the ten toes stage, the time of ten kingdoms.

As it is briefly explained above, the unique character of the ceramic clay type of democracy opposes the destructive beastly character of iron. Instead, it upholds human rights of the people because "all men are created equal." This phrase from the Declaration of Independence of the United States of America teaches the truth that all men are created by God and equal before Him. Nations that does not recognize this premise cannot belong to the ceramic clay type of democracy. The nations of ceramic type of democracy are also the nations in which the mystery Kingdom of God will be in full operation in due time. The mystery Kingdom of God is the preliminary Kingdom of God among us through the Holy Spirit prior to the arrival of the Kingdom itself on earth.

Of course, no one denies that Great Britain will belong to the ceramic clay type, but let us hope that Great Britain as well as all other nations that will belong to the 'Axis of God,' is renewed before the 'ten kingdom stage' arrives. In fact, calling the people by 'citizens' or 'subjects' is only a trivial and technical matter. What is important though for the nations is that they should be operating in the realm of the mystery kingdom by walking in the Spirit. This may sound very idealistic but such renewal time is impending as we approach the harvest time. This is the time when the words spoken through Paul in Ephesians 5:25-27, will be realized. "Christ loved the church and gave Himself for it, that He might sanctify and cleanse it with the washing of water by the word, that He might present it to Himself a glorious church, not having spot or wrinkle or any such thing, but that it should be holy and without blemish." So far, we have not seen a church as such. Nevertheless, the Church Age will never come to an end until these words are fulfilled.

Some may wonder if the ceramic clay symbolizes the democratic form of governments and the Scripture tells them to be weaker than iron, how can the 'Axis of God' which will be composed of the ceramic clay type of nations can sustain themselves against the iron type of nations which are supposed to be the allies of Antichrist, the 'Axis of Evil.'

The First Corinthians 1:25 says that the weakness of God is stronger than men. I Corinthians 15:43 also says that it is sown in weakness; it is raised in power. The Second Corinthians 12:9 says that the Lord told Paul personally, "My grace is sufficient for you, for My strength is made perfect in weakness." Paul also testified, "He was crucified in weakness, but He lives by the power of God. For we also are weak in Him, but we shall live with Him by the power of God toward you."

We can also read how the grace of God can turn the weakness of believer into His power in the scene that described how God will defend Jerusalem when the nations besiege the city to destroy it at the end of the tribulation. Zechariah 12:8 says, "In that day the Lord will defend the inhabitants of Jerusalem; the one who is feeble among them in that day shall be like David, and the house of David shall be like **God**, like **'the Angel of the Lord'** before them. 'It shall be in that day that I will seek to destroy all the nations that come against Jerusalem.'" (In Old Testament, 'the Angel of the Lord' signifies Jesus Christ.)

Unless we are humble and weak, God cannot operate in us. In order to be able to operate in God's power we, by all means, need to dwell in humility and weakness.

The world history is now unfolding to reveal its destiny at an accelerated pace and in an unprecedented manner. God is speaking to us today through the series of disasters such as, the 9/11 attacks, the Tsunami of 2004 and Katrina of New Orleans and so on.

Hebrews 12:26-29 also says:

"Yet once more I shake not only the earth, but also heaven." Now this, 'yet once more,' indicates the removal of those things that are being shaken, as of things that is made, that the things which cannot be shaken may remain. Therefore, since we are receiving a kingdom which cannot be shaken, let us have grace, by which we may serve God acceptably with reverence and godly fear. For our God is a consuming fire.

(Hebrews 12:26-29)

We still have time for repentance because Jesus said in Matthew 24:6-14,

> "And you will hear of wars and rumors of wars. See that you are not troubled; for all these things must come to pass, but the end is not yet. For nation will rise against nation, and kingdom against kingdom. And there will be famines, pestilences, and earthquakes in various places. All these are the beginning of sorrows.
>
> "Then they will deliver you up to tribulation and kill you, and you will be hated by all nations for My name's sake. And then many will be offended, will betray one another, and will hate one another. Then many false prophets will rise up and deceive many. And because lawlessness will abound, the love of many will grow cold. But he who endures to the end shall be saved. And the gospel of the kingdom will be preached in all the world as a witness to all the nations, and then the end will come."
>
> (Matt. 24:6-14)

However, He said in v. 34, "Assuredly, I say to you, this generation will by no means pass away till all these things are fulfilled."

Now, we need to know this generation about which Jesus spoke to His disciples on the Mount of Olives has already begun, and will not pass away till all these things are fulfilled. As Jesus said, the generation has started with the rumors of wars. 'Nation against nation and kingdom against kingdom' is said to be the Hebrew expression for the worldwide global war. We often think of worldwide wars in terms of World War I and World War II, but they were only local wars in the sense of the global war that Matthew chapter 24 referred. 'The war against terror' declared by Bush administration after the 9/11 attacks seems to be developing more like a worldwide global war in the Scriptural sense. We are, however, consoled somewhat because Jesus said, "See that you are not troubled; for all these things must come to pass, but the end is not yet."

Jesus in addition to the worldwide global war also warned against the natural calamities such as, famines, pestilences and earthquakes in various places. The 'Tsunami' of 2004 certainly was an unprecedented earthquake underneath the ocean encompassing two largest continents in the world, the Asian and the African. Katrina of New Orleans of 2005 was also an unprecedented hurricane in the United States history. The U.S. government has also allocated 7 billion dollars to protect American citizens from the imminent pestilence of avian flu. We understand that the coming of avian flu is no more a matter of 'if' but 'when.'

But, Jesus said that all these are the beginning of sorrows. The events of the 9/11attacks, the Tsunami, and Katrina of New Orleans are the beginning of sorrows, but the end time will not be too long because the history of the world seems to be unfolding rather rapidly. We still have time for repentance but not for lingering on to the sinful life. The warning to the sinful life of the world should be the church's prime task among the works that the church must take on in these latter days. Or, we may have to face the 'terror of the Lord' with even harsher severity as He shakes the earth and heavens as Isaiah 2:10 said, "Enter into the rock, and hide in the dust, from the terror of the Lord and the glory of His majesty.

While the 'Axis of God' is formed and consolidated in the Northeast Asian bloc, the unified Korea will develop strong ties with Israel by cooperating in various fields, such as, trades, businesses, cultural matters, military matters, scientific research, and so on. Through the cooperation between the two nations, Korea will be able to consolidate her position to carry out the assigned role for the Holy One of Israel.

Ezekiel chapter 37 tells of the vision of dry bones. The dry bones in the prophecy symbolize Israel in exile. This prophecy is for Israel's resuscitation and its fulfillment in the Kingdom after the tribulation in the end days. Also note that Israel's life of Diaspora will not end until the Kingdom is established on the earth. The followings are the excerpts from Ezekiel chapter 37:

The Vision of Dry Bones:

The hand of the Lord came upon me and brought me out in the Spirit of the Lord, and set me down in the midst of the valley; and it was full of bones.

'Thus says the Lord God to these bones: "Surely I will cause breath to enter into you, and you shall live… " '

So I prophesied as I was commanded; and as I prophesied, there was a noise, and suddenly a rattling; and the bones came together, bone to bone.

Then He said to me, "Prophesy to the breath, prophesy, son of man, and say to the breath, 'thus says the Lord God: "Come from the four winds,
O breath, and breath on these slain, that they may live." ' "

So I prophesied as He commanded me, and breath came into them, and they lived, and stood upon their feet, an exceedingly great army.

Then He said to me, "Son of man, these bones are the whole house of Israel. They indeed say, 'Our bones are dry, our hope is lost, and we ourselves are cut off!' "

"Therefore prophesy and say to them, 'Thus says the Lord God: "Behold, O My people, I will open your graves and cause you to come up from your graves, and bring you into the land of Israel. Then you shall know that I am the Lord, when I have opened your graves, O My people, and brought you up from your graves. I will put My Spirit in you, and you shall live, and I will place you in your own land. Then you shall know that I, the Lord, have spoken it and performed it," says the Lord." ' "

(From Ezekiel 37:1-14)

Sign of the Two Sticks

Again the word of the Lord came to me saying, "As for you, son of man, take a stick for yourself and write on it: 'For Judah and for the children of Israel, his companions.' Then take another stick and write on it, 'For Joseph, the stick of Ephraim, and for all the house of Israel, his companions.' Then join them one to another for yourself into one stick, and they will become one in your hand. . .'"

"Then say to them, 'Thus says the Lord God: "Surely I will take the children of Israel from among the nations, wherever they have gone, and will gather them from every side and bring them into their own land; and I will make them one nation in the land, on the mountains of Israel; and one king shall be king over them all; they shall no longer be two nations, nor shall they ever be divided into two kingdoms again.

"They shall not defile themselves anymore with their idols, nor with their detestable things, nor with any of their transgressions; but I will deliver them from all their dwelling places in which they have sinned, and will cleanse them. Then they shall be My people, and I will be their God. David My servant shall be king over them, and they shall all have one shepherd; they shall also walk in My judgments and observe My statutes, and do them.

"Then they shall dwell in the land that I have given to Jacob My servant, where your fathers dwelt; and they shall dwell there, they, their children, and their children's children, forever; and My servant David shall be their prince forever.

"Moreover I will make a covenant of peace with them, and it shall be an everlasting covenant with them; I will establish them and multiply them, and I will set My sanctuary in their midst forevermore. My tabernacle also shall be with them; indeed I will be their God, and they shall be My people. The nations also will know that I, the Lord, sanctify Israel, when My sanctuary is in their midst forevermore." ' "

(From Ezekiel 37:15-28)

Israel has been in exile due especially to her sin of Idol worship. It began far back from the time of King Solomon. Israel was divided into two kingdoms soon after King Solomon died because he had gone after Ashtoreth the goddess of Sidonians and Milcom the god of the Ammonites while he was still a king. The northern kingdom was called Israel and the southern kingdom, Judah. The northern kingdom Israel was taken exile to Assyria when it fell in B.C. 722 and it was followed by Judah to Babylon when it fell in B.C. 586. Although Judah had once returned to Jerusalem, it was taken again to exile in A.D. 135 after she refused to accept Jesus Christ as their Messiah.

God then showed Ezekiel how He will bring Israel that had been torn apart, back together with the sign of two sticks. We know that God has already begun to resuscitate the dry bones to life again. The emerging of the Messianic Jews throughout the nineteenth century in Great Britain and the United States, and the establishment of the Jewish state in Palestine on May 14, 1948 after World War II can be taken as a sign of the beginning of her resuscitation.

The process will continue to take place until Israel finally as a nation is regenerated in the Spirit. This will occur at the end of the great tribulation in Jerusalem according to the Scripture. This is the time when the New Covenant which began on the day of Pentecost will be concluded. Then, there will be the united Israel in His hand in the Kingdom.

To Israel which is so immersed today in the idol of humanism, the prophecies are mere words and they cannot believe them. They need to see realization of an amazing renewal in the Gentile nation before she comes to believe in what God has spoken of Israel. This is part of God's plan for Israel's salvation.

Alas, the nation on the Korean peninsula has been divided after World War II. The cause of its division is believed by the Christians of the land to be their sin of idolatry to the Shinto God during the Japanese occupation. If this were true, the cause would be the same as that of Israel's division, the idol worship.

The Lord, however, will soon join one to another to make the divided Korea once again whole in His hand for Israel to see. God indeed will show Israelites how He will bring the divided nation of Korea together in His hand so that Israel may believe that God can do the same for Israel.

Although the prophecy of Ezekiel chapter 37 is about Israel's unification and restoration, it also is applicable to the divided nation of Korea just as Paul applied the prophecies in Hosea which was for Israel, to the conversion of Gentiles on the basis of the similar situation of two peoples.

The prophecies in Hosea which says, "I will call them 'My people' who were not my people, and her beloved who was not beloved. And it shall come to pass in the place where it was said to them, 'You are not My people, 'there they will be called sons of the living God," promise to restore the lost position of the Israel as the 'people of God.' These prophecies of Hosea could be applied to the conversion of Gentiles because the Gentiles too were expecting to become the 'people of God' as much as the Jewish people want to have their position to be restored. Both of them were looking forward to the same goal of becoming the 'people of God.'

The cross of Jesus Christ has not only made it possible for Israel to have her position restored by accepting Jesus as their Messiah, but also for the Gentiles to attain the honorable new position as 'the people of God.' when they accept Jesus as their Lord.

By the same token, the prophecy of the 'sign of two sticks' in chapter 37 of Ezekiel can be applied to the Gentile nation of Korea, because she also shares with Israel the desire and the respective roles to bring about the Kingdom on earth.

Israel will return to Christ only when she sees and touches and feels the nation that has become 'the people of God' by accepting Him as their Lord. The nation of Korea that has been made whole in God's hand will be righteous, rich, and powerful by embracing God's justice and love. There shall be no more lies, lewdness, worship of money or suchlike in that nation. Then, Israel will know that the Lord will perform as He has spoken, and He shall do the same even more thoroughly in Israel and the rest of the world in the Kingdom.

Israel will surely return to her Messiah Jesus. In that day, the nations will know that the Lord sanctifies Israel, when His sanctuary is in their midst forevermore!

Bibliography:

1. Schaff, P. *History of the Christian Church*, vol. V. Hendrickson Publishers, 1996. .

2, Tregelles, Samuel P. *Gesenius' Hebrew-Chaldee Lexicon to the Old Testament.* WM. B. Eedmans Publishing Co. Grand Rapids, Michigan, 1980.

3. Paik, Lak-Geoon George. *The History of Protestant Missions in Korea 1832-1910,* Yonsei University Press, 1998.

About the Authors

Young Gil Gohng was born in Seoul, Korea, and educated at Johns Hopkins University. Upon his return to Korea, he founded a manufacturing firm and worked as the CEO of the corporation. His wife Therese who is now with the Lord, was a librarian trained at Vilanova University in Philadelphia.

He and his wife were both good Christians and had been actively participating in the Spiritual renewal movement at a local church when they realized that God was speaking to them through Jeremiah 33:3. The verse which says, "Call to Me, and I will answer you and show you great and mighty things which you do not know" prompted them to call to Him in search of what He promised. As a result, they could write a book titled "Call unto Me!" with what they learned from the Lord during their search for Him. What they received from the Lord then was elucidation of Deuteronomy 32:21 and it was about a nation that will arouse Israel to godly jealousy so that she may lead Israel to Jesus Christ. "Why Korea? -*The Unification of Korea & the Church's Mission to Israel*" is also an outcome of His elucidation on the verse.

Young Gil Gohng also wrote two exegetic books, one on the Gospel of John and the other one on The First Letter of John. These books were written in Korean. He is also the father of two daughters Mary and Ann, and a son Yohan.

Where to go when you have questions:

Write also to <siloamwords@yahoo.com> for any question on what is written in the book or in the Holy Scripture.

Lightning Source UK Ltd.
Milton Keynes UK
UKHW011251280721
387870UK00001B/9